PUFFIN BOOKS

STOLEN HISTORY

STOLEN
HISTORY

THE TRUTH ABOUT THE BRITISH EMPIRE
AND HOW IT SHAPED US

SATHNAM
SANGHERA

Illustrated by Jen Khatun

PUFFIN

PUFFIN BOOKS

UK | USA | Canada | Ireland | Australia
India | New Zealand | South Africa

Puffin Books is part of the Penguin Random House group of companies
whose addresses can be found at global.penguinrandomhouse.com.

www.penguin.co.uk
www.puffin.co.uk
www.ladybird.co.uk

Penguin
Random House
UK

First published by Puffin Books 2023

002

Text design by Janene Spencer

Printed in Great Britain by Clays Ltd, Elcograf S.p.A.

The authorized representative in the EEA is Penguin Random House Ireland,
Morrison Chambers, 32 Nassau Street, Dublin D02 YH68

A CIP catalogue record for this book is available from the British Library

ISBN: 978–0–241–62343–5

All correspondence to:
Puffin Books, Penguin Random House Children's
One Embassy Gardens, 8 Viaduct Gardens, London SW11 7BW

MIX
Paper from
responsible sources
FSC® C018179

Penguin Random House is committed to a
sustainable future for our business, our readers
and our planet. This book is made from Forest
Stewardship Council® certified paper.

My thanks to Lottie Moggach,
Kit Moggach, Phoebe Jascourt,
Corinne Fowler, Shalina Patel,
Anita Anand, Kate Teltscher,
Kim Wagner and Alan Lester.

A MAP OF THE WORLD IN 1919

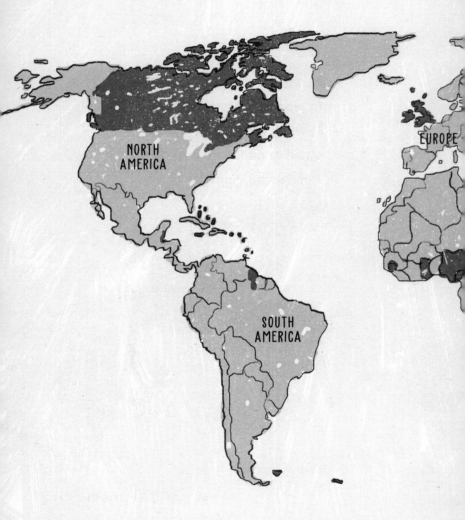

NORTH
AMERICA

SOUTH
AMERICA

EUROPE

Source: Adam Taylor, *Washington Post*. 'Map: The Rise and Fall of the British Empire', 8 September 2015. Accessed January 2023.

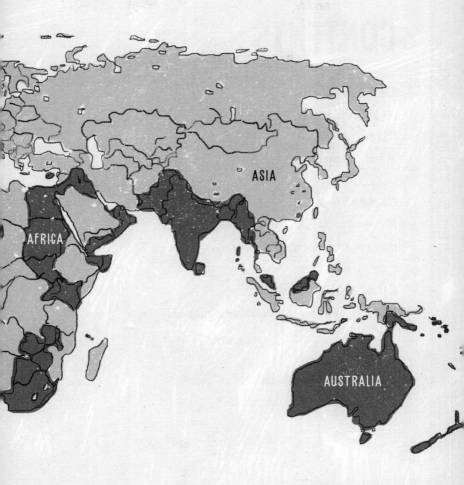

ASIA

AFRICA

AUSTRALIA

COLONIZED BY BRITAIN

CONTENTS

INTRODUCTION

History bored me to tears at school. I couldn't see how spending a whole term learning about the Stone Age was going to help me live my life. It must have been grim to be those strange hairy people in those strange and hairy times, but I didn't understand why we needed to know about them. I mean, we had chainsaws instead of stone tools, we lived in houses rather than caves, and we had fantastically cheap razors available in most supermarkets. Nor did I see how the Hundred Years War had any relevance to us. Beyond the fact that every single lesson on it felt like it was 116 years long (which was, in fact, how long the Hundred Years War actually lasted. How did the war-naming person get that so wrong?!).

It wasn't just history I struggled with. I never got the hang of art; everything I ever drew ended up looking like a donkey. And I dreaded cross-country running. Not only were we told to run for six kilometres without stopping or drinking water, but the teachers also threatened that we'd have to run in our underpants if we 'forgot' our running kits (the 1980s were weird!). But history was dreadful. It comes as a massive surprise therefore that, at the age of forty-six, I am the author of a bestselling history book for adults, *Empireland*. It's even more of a shock that here I am now, beginning a children's version of that book.

Until recently I had read very few history books – finding them, in general, too long and boring. I'm not a historian; I'm a journalist and author. And I didn't even study history beyond the age of sixteen. What changed? Well, it turns out there's an incredibly interesting slice of history which I wasn't taught about at school or university – the British Empire. It's a part of history that is still important to life as we know it today. It explains so much about Britain as a nation, including where some of our money comes from, the stuff we find in our museums, the reason the country is home to citizens of all different races and backgrounds, the food we eat, the words we use and so much more.

It's this history that explains lots about my life too, such as the reasons why my Indian parents emigrated to Britain in the 1960s ('emigrate' means moving from one country to another). It also explains the racism that surrounded me as I grew up in Wolverhampton in the 1980s and 1990s. For example, at the time certain jobs seemed closed off to people of colour – not just the fancy jobs running companies, but some non-white people even found themselves unable to get jobs as teachers or drivers. Some pubs and clubs didn't allow entry to those who had a different skin colour to white British citizens. And there was horrible abuse and violence directed at those who weren't white.

I bet the history of the British Empire explains something about your life too.

The British Empire (and don't worry, I'll be explaining exactly what this is very soon!) was the biggest empire in human history, covering a quarter of the planet at its height, and is the biggest thing Britain ever did as a nation. It's as important as the leading role we played in the Second World War, when we beat the evil German Nazis, and cemented the idea that we were as plucky and determined as the British bulldog that is sometimes

4

used to symbolize us (and which graces the cover of this book). Frankly, it's one of the biggest things that ever happened in the history of the world.

It's astonishing that I was taught almost nothing about it at school. And it's astounding that it's still not a priority to teach this in history classes today. So do not fear if you've not come across it yet either. It turns out we're not alone. In my research and conversations, I've come across adults who studied history at some of the most famous universities in Britain who learned almost nothing about the British Empire. A survey conducted around twenty-five years ago found that huge numbers of adults had very little knowledge about it. For example, more than half the people taking part didn't know that the USA began as a British project. We can't be blamed for Hershey's chocolate, or take credit for Disneyland – it was long before all those things – but, yes, America was once a British enterprise.

If you didn't know these things either, there's no shame in it at all; you're still at school and learning. Also, I hope you'll feel a lot more knowledgeable by the time you get to the end of this book. The plan is to tell you some of the things I wish I had known at your age (beyond a shortcut to that dreaded cross-country route!). I'll explain what the British Empire was exactly and why lots of us don't know more about it. We'll talk about museums, which are home to many priceless artefacts belonging to countries that used to be part of the British Empire. I'll give you examples of things in our modern world that have roots in the empire – things we see, do, say and experience, from Britain's towns and cities to our food and drink, sports, books, plants and more. And we'll also discuss what you can do to expand and spread your knowledge and understanding about it.

Most importantly, I'll tell you how the British Empire explains why modern Britain is such a multicultural place, filled with lots of people of different colours and cultures and walks of life, living alongside each other. It's a lot to aim for, but I hope that by the end of this book you'll understand what has taken me forty-six years to discover: that if we learn the truth about our past, we can make better sense of the present and future. And also fight for a kinder and fairer world.

(The one thing I definitely won't be doing, however, is the illustrations. The talented Jen Khatun is in charge of those, which means that if you see something that resembles a donkey, it is actually meant to be a donkey.)

CHAPTER 1

What on earth was the
British Empire?

Let's start with the basics. What is an 'empire'? You've probably heard the word before, perhaps in connection with the Roman Empire, or the song by Jay-Z and Alicia Keys, 'Empire State of Mind', or the Star Wars film *The Empire Strikes Back*. Or maybe, even, with the British Empire, which is the one we're interested in here.

An empire is a group of countries that are ruled by a single other country or government. There are other words that are useful to know, as they come up a lot when discussing empires. You'll see these words appear many times throughout the book, so I've created a short dictionary for you to come back to whenever you need it:

- **Imperialism:** this is the practice of creating an empire (for instance, you might come across the phrase 'Britain's imperial past', which means when Britain had an empire).

- **Colonialism:** if one country takes control of another, it colonizes it. If one nation of people takes over another nation of people, the people who are conquering are colonizers and the people who are conquered are colonized. The taken-over place is now a colony, and the people who came in to do the 'taking over' are colonists or colonialists.

The words mean quite similar things. If this seems like it's already getting complicated, don't worry. There's no getting away from the fact that the British Empire can be a fiendishly tricky subject. More complicated than algebra and the poems of William Shakespeare and the plot of *The Lord of the Rings* and the storyline of *The Legend of Zelda: Breath of the Wild* combined. But that doesn't mean we shouldn't learn about it. Britain's colonial past is important to understand.

So why would a country want to have an empire? There are three BIG reasons: power, money and glory.

The more land and resources that you control (such as another country's food and valuable materials), the stronger, more famous and wealthier you are and the more adventures you have. Unsurprisingly, lots of rulers through history have been keen to have an empire. One of the most famous empires was the Roman Empire, which began in 27 BC and continued for around 500 years. During this time, the Romans colonized large parts of Europe and beyond, including Britain. (In fact, the Romans weren't the only ones who colonized Britain – the Vikings, the Saxons and the Normans all had a go at it too.)

It's generally accepted that Britain's empire began back in the 1600s during the reign of Elizabeth I, when seafaring adventurers 'discovered'* lands rich in highly prized goods. It existed for about 500 years and over time many other European countries, such as France, the Netherlands (also known as Holland), Portugal, Spain and Italy, have had their own empires too. Britain's empire, though, was the biggest there has ever been. It was seven times the size of the mighty Roman Empire.

At its peak, around a century ago, the British Empire covered 13.71 million square miles, and included India (sometimes also referred to as 'the subcontinent'),

---

* The people who already lived in these parts of the world (who are called 'indigenous') would quite rightly object to this word, given they'd been aware of their own homelands before the British imperialists turned up. Imagine how annoyed you'd be if a random person came round to your house and then went around declaring to everyone that they'd somehow 'discovered' it. You were aware of it first! It didn't need discovering!

several countries in Africa, Canada, Australia, and numerous Caribbean islands. That is a quarter of all the land in the world. Or to put it another, even more mind-boggling way, if all Britain's empire in the early 1900s was put together, it would cover almost the entire surface of the moon! Because it spanned so many different countries and time zones across the globe, it was said that, at its height, you could travel through Britain's empire without seeing the sun set.

The British ended up with different colonies for all sorts of different reasons. For example, Britain initially became involved in India because the country was rich in resources that it wanted to trade, and Britain saw Australia as a useful place to send prisoners who had committed crimes.

British imperialism went through many different phases. At one time it was acceptable for white men to marry the brown women they met in the empire. But then, at another, interracial relationships were frowned upon. At one stage British imperialists worked hard to stamp out the evils of the slave trade wherever they encountered it. But then there was a long period between the late seventeenth and early nineteenth centuries when the British Empire profited from the evils of the Atlantic slave trade. This involved taking Black men, women and children who had been kidnapped from countries across Africa and shipping them across the Atlantic Ocean to force them to work, for free, on farms across the Caribbean, North America and elsewhere. More than 3 million people from the continent of Africa suffered this fate during the British Empire, with many of them dying on the journey due to terrible conditions on the ships. The sugar and other crops produced by the enslaved made some British people very rich, but eventually Britain accepted the trade was evil, outlawed it and took a leading role in abolishing (which means ending) it around the world.

So how was such a collection of countries controlled?

Well, think of your school. If it's like most schools, it probably has a number of classes of a similar size that are normally calm and well behaved (OK, that part might not be true, but stick with me here!). The class teachers probably follow the national curriculum that has been set by the government to plan their lessons. And, at the top of it all, in charge of everything, there is a wise, kind and efficient head teacher. Well, Britain's empire was absolutely nothing like that at all!

Now imagine instead that each class at your school is a completely different size: some tiny, some huge. Imagine that it takes many months to transfer messages between the head teacher and classrooms. Imagine that some classes are fairly peaceful, while some are out of control and violent. Imagine there are no school rules and no national curriculum and that, although there is a head teacher, they rarely get involved. Instead it is up to each class teacher to set the rules and lessons for their class, and so all the classes do different things in a different way. Some of these teachers know what they are doing but others don't. Some are nice, and want to help the children, but others are cruel. Some of them are so lazy and mean that they make their pupils do all their work for them, while punishing them and taking all the payment and credit. THAT'S how the empire was run.

Sounds pretty chaotic, doesn't it? And it often was. But for centuries it survived and thrived. It made Britain the most powerful nation on Earth, and gave us lots of things that remain part of our lives today.

Most importantly, the empire is largely responsible for making Britain the multicultural country it is today.

Many British people of African, Caribbean, South Asian and South-East Asian background are here because Britain colonized these parts of the world. They probably include some of your friends, as well as famous people such as Marcus Rashford MBE. (By the way, do you know what 'MBE' stands for? Member of the Most Excellent Order of the British Empire!) They might well include you.

Marcus Rashford and sugar are undeniably brilliant additions to Britain (although your dentist may disagree with the second), but the British Empire remains a hugely controversial subject. People have been arguing for centuries about whether it was a good or bad thing (spoiler alert – it's not as simple as that), but pretty much every other aspect of it is argued over too. If you can possibly imagine it, people argue about it more intensely than you've ever argued with your friends about Pokémon card swaps, Superman v Spider-Man, who is the best YouTuber, who is best at dancing/cartwheels, or who has the best trainers.

Given that the British Empire involved the enslavement of millions and the deaths of millions of others through famine, war and disease, it's no surprise that tempers can rise when the topic is discussed. Lots of conversations about the British Empire involve at least one person getting very upset or shouting, and another person getting very defensive. There are, however, some things people do agree on – or, rather, can talk about without getting too furious. For instance, it is generally accepted that its great power came to an end in the twentieth century, when India declared its independence from Britain in 1947, and when Hong Kong was handed back to the Chinese in 1997. People also cannot deny that the empire has shaped Britain in all sorts of ways – not only in the little things that fill our everyday lives, but in the way British people see themselves and how they see the rest of the world.

Often we don't realize the impact the empire continues to have on our lives, and how many things that we say, do, see and believe stem from this history.

NUTMEG

As we now know, the British Empire started when seafaring adventurers became aware of 'new' islands and nations overflowing with valuable products and wanted control over them. One of the first – and most interesting – of those lands was a tiny island called Run in what is now Indonesia. And when I say tiny, I mean TINY. Run is only two miles long and half a mile wide, which means you could walk – or run! – across the whole place in your lunch break.

But what Run lacks in size, it makes up for in . . . nutmeg trees. Nutmeg is a spice that you've probably eaten yourself if you've ever enjoyed a gingerbread man or certain curries and

pastas. Hundreds of years ago the island and its neighbours were the world's main source of nutmeg. And given food and drink in Britain at the time was often beige and boring, nutmeg was incredibly sought after. It was so valuable, in fact, that nutmeg bought in Run could be sold on in Britain for 600 times the price. So if you bought £2-worth of nutmeg with your pocket money on the island of Run, you could have sold it for £1,200 in Britain!

It's no wonder that Britain was interested in controlling Run. But so were the Dutch. Much squabbling between British and Dutch traders followed, and eventually the islanders of Run decided they would rather work with the British. The Dutch weren't happy about this and decided to blockade the island – which means they sealed it off to stop goods or people from entering or leaving. Eventually the British lost interest in Run, and in 1667 agreed a deal with the Dutch. The British would give them the island and, in return, the Dutch would give Britain an island they had colonized on the North American coast, which was then called New Amsterdam.

King Charles II gave the American island to his brother James, Duke of York (later James II), and the settlement was renamed after him. Can you see where this is going? Yes – in exchange for tiny little Run and its nutmeg trees, the British got New York City, which is now one of the largest and most famous cities on the planet!

THE EAST INDIA COMPANY

If you've ever been in central London, you may have passed a shop called the East India Company. You probably didn't even notice it. It mostly sells expensive tea and extremely expensive tea accessories. Fancy a tea humidor? Well, after you've looked up what a 'humidor' is – like I just did – you will probably decide that you'd rather not pay £10,500 for an airtight container to keep tea fresh.

The story behind the shop's name, however, is really interesting. The East India Company was a British company that played a hugely important part in Britain's empire, but

sometimes behaved shockingly. It was established in 1600 to trade in silk and spices from Asia. The company was soon given extraordinary powers by the British government, allowing it to colonize and run countries, most notably India. It printed its own money and it had its own military force, which was twice the size of the British army. Imagine if Nando's suddenly had a massive army and was able to take over other countries! Sounds crazy, right?

But with its vast power, the East India Company became greedy. It illegally sold opium, a dangerous drug, to China, which killed many people and destroyed many lives. Also, in the seventeenth and eighteenth centuries, it traded in products that relied on slave labour. It took advantage of India's workers and products - including fabrics - and made its own officials incredibly rich, while making Indian people pay high taxes, often when they couldn't afford to pay them. And its cruel policies led to terrible famines, such as the one in Bengal in 1770 in which millions died. After all these scandals, and many others too, the original East

India Company was finally shut down in 1874 and the British government took over its territories and army.

The shops with this name today aren't the same business – but they rely on its reputation to sell their products. Considering the original company's dark and violent history, it's a strange decision. The owner of the new East India Company is Indian himself, and so you might think that he wouldn't want to use the name of a company that harmed and robbed his mother country. But, as we'll soon discover, even at the time there were many Indians who supported the original East India Company. I told you that the empire could be complicated.

The fact that these shops exist, and people buy things from them, tells us that some people might look back fondly on the British Empire. Perhaps these customers would love to go back to the days when Britain ruled a quarter of the planet. In the meantime, they'll have to make do with a cup of VERY expensive tea.

THE SCOUTS

Dyb dyb dyb! Dob dob dob! This might look like a string of nonsense words, but it's something that used to be chanted by the Scouts – a movement that sprang directly from the British Empire.

The organization was the bright idea of a military man called Lord Baden-Powell, who became a hero during a war between British and Dutch settlers (called Boers) in what is now South Africa between 1899 and 1902. A few years later, he decided to start the Boy Scouts, with the aim of teaching boys how to be good, well-rounded citizens and, more specifically, good imperialists. Baden-Powell wanted to create a new generation of children fit to run the empire properly, and better than other European empires, such as those run by the Dutch, Belgians and French. In fact, he originally wanted to call the movement 'the Imperial Scouts'!

Along with teaching the importance of values such as patriotism (which means taking pride in your country), obedience, teamwork, a sense of purpose and self-reliance, there was also a focus on outdoor activities such as camping, sailing, archery, hiking and survival skills. Badges were awarded when a boy mastered a new skill. Some of these were straightforward skills, like cooking or first aid, while some were a little more unusual. You could get a badge for bell-ringing, bookbinding and even chicken farming! If you're a Scout nowadays, you might be awarded badges for anything from life-saving skills to writing and astronomy. One of their mottos was 'Be Prepared', which came from the initials of the founder,

Baden-Powell. There were secret greetings and in-jokes, as well as funny rituals, such as shaking hands with your left hand rather than the more usual right hand, and making a three-finger salute (with your palm facing outwards, fold your thumb and little finger in and stick the remaining fingers up). I've just tried it with a passing postman and it's harder than it sounds!

The movement was a wild success, first in Britain and then around the world. At the very first Scout meeting in 1907, twenty boys went camping. Two years later, there were 100,000 members. And within twenty years there were 2 million in seventy-eight countries. Baden-Powell's handbook, *Scouting for Boys*, became one of the bestselling books of all time.

In 1910, girls were demanding to participate in the Boy Scouts, and so the Girl Guides movement began. In 1912, along with his sister, Baden-Powell wrote a handbook for the Girl Guides, which was subtitled *How Girls Can Help Build the Empire.* Today the Scouts movement isn't as huge as it was, but it's still going strong. Nowadays girls can be Scouts too. You might even be a member yourself. In which case, all together now: Dyb dyb dyb! (which stands for 'Do your best!') Dob dob dob! ('Do our best!').

CHAPTER 2

If it was such a big part of history, why don't we know more about it?

You're probably starting to wonder, if the British Empire was so massive, if it lasted for so long, if it affected so many people and if it gets people so furious, then why haven't you heard about it?

Why haven't your parents or teachers tried to teach you about it? Why are you only reading about it now?

It has been a long time since I was a kid, but I still remember how annoying it was when adults avoided certain subjects. It was particularly annoying when they used complicated words and phrases so they didn't have to answer difficult questions. And while it's not quite the same thing as failing to explain why your favourite guinea pig died, or why you can't, as a ten-year-old, drive the family car to Aberdeen, or why you can't stay up until 4 a.m. watching *Trollhunters*, something similar often happens when people talk about the British Empire.

When the topic comes up, people have a tendency to change the subject or drift into 'euphemisms' (these are polite or mild words used instead of words that might be considered harsh or blunt, but this means they hide the real meaning of things). For example, take the *Oxford Dictionary of National Biography*, which is essentially a list of the most famous Britons to have ever lived. It includes stories of men and women who owned enslaved people during the empire, but it has a history of trying to avoid mentioning the topic of slavery. Instead, it has distracted readers with phrases (or euphemisms) like these, to make it seem less severe:

- **'plantation owner'** – a plantation is a large farm that usually specializes in just one crop. Typically labourers live and work on a plantation. 'Plantation owner' is a euphemism for someone who ran large farms where enslaved people lived and did most of the hard work.

- **'West Indies merchant'** – this is a euphemism for someone who made money by selling the

produce farmed by the enslaved, and possibly
by trading in enslaved people too.

- **'plantation agriculture'** – meaning the
  industry that produced crops through the
  brutal enforcement of work by the enslaved
  people. The enslaved people were seen as the
  property of their owners and were treated
  horrendously.

- **'possessed considerable property in
  Jamaica'** – this is another way of saying that
  the person owned a load of plantations, as well
  as the enslaved people who often worked on
  the properties. They almost certainly became
  very rich through forcing the enslaved people
  to perform hard labour.

What these phrases hide is that during the British
Empire Britain transported more than 3 million
enslaved people from Africa, causing unimaginable
pain and suffering for many, many years. Sadly this is
still felt today by the generations that came after. And
this brings us to the first of many reasons why we tend

not to hear or learn about this part of Britain's history. There was a huge amount of cruelty and suffering brought upon African people by British imperialists, which can make it painful or embarrassing, and therefore very difficult, for many people to talk about. This difficulty can lead to something called 'selective amnesia'.

Selective amnesia

'Amnesia' means memory loss, so selective amnesia means either deliberately or unconsciously choosing to forget some things that might be unpleasant and remembering only the good. And there are plenty more instances of this in relation to the British Empire. One key example is the railways of India. Lots of British people feel proud that thousands of miles of railways were built in India during the empire and that these railways still function today. This pride is reflected in the many British TV programmes on the subject. But the truth that is often deliberately forgotten is that the railways were built for the British people, not the Indian population who had been colonized. These railways allowed the British to transport things more easily out of the country for sale, and meant that they could move armies quickly if Indians rebelled against the empire. It's also worth noting that the hard work of building them was done by Indians (an estimated 25,000 Indians lost their lives while constructing railway sections over two particularly steep mountain passes over an eight-year-long project). And indigenous Indians weren't even allowed to do the most important jobs on the trains. At one stage of the empire, Sikhs like my family were not seen as trustworthy or capable enough to drive the trains, even though they were trusted enough to fight for the British Empire in large numbers in both world wars. All this discrimination, danger and death involved in the Indian railways is difficult, painful, and very upsetting for people to reflect on. ('Discrimination' means treating someone in a different and worse way because of, for example, their skin colour or their religion.) It's much easier for TV shows to focus on the parts that make it look like a positive tale.

Anger

As well as forgetfulness, there also tends to be quite a lot of anger when painful, yet completely true, facts about the British Empire are pointed out. For example, I try my best to offer the full complicated truth about Britain's imperial history when I write and speak on radio and TV. While I resist covering up the horrific facts of slavery, and the pain and suffering caused by colonization, I also explore what some may consider to be the positive legacies of empire. I try very hard to be fair, but I still often receive sweary letters in the post, and have had people turning up at my events to shout at me for 'insulting' British history. I've even had hundreds of offensive racist social media comments telling me to 'go back to where I came from' (I will talk more about phrases like this – and how to respond to them – in Chapter 7).

And it's not just me who gets told off for talking about this. Have you ever seen a show called *Horrible Histories*? This programme is based on a series of books for children about different moments in history. In one episode Queen Victoria discovers that many of the things she enjoys that she thought were British actually have foreign roots. She finds out, for instance, that her British tea is from India ('Yes, for your cuppa thousands died and many wars were fought.'), that her sugar is from the Caribbean ('For sugar in your cup of tea, slavery's been supported.'), that her British-manufactured cotton vest is made from cotton from America and picked by enslaved people again ('Your empire's built on fighting wars, that's how your income's swollen.'), and, in conclusion, that a striking number of her 'British things are from abroad and most are frankly stolen'. This is all basically true, but the show received tons of complaints about it. 'Is the BBC on a mission to get itself closed down?' one person asked. 'This is anti-British drivel of a high order,' claimed another.

Why do true facts about the British Empire inspire angry responses like these? I think it's partly because the British Empire happened abroad. Even at the time of the empire, it was possible for British people to pretend it didn't exist. Having to face up to the brutal facts can be, for some, surprising and difficult. It's no wonder that people don't talk about it very much . . .

It's personal

Others don't want to talk about it because it feels raw and personal to them, as they had family members who were involved in empire. Perhaps their ancestors were themselves colonizers or slave owners, and the present-day person feels embarrassed about it. Or perhaps their ancestors played a role in running the empire, and they believe that they were good people but are worried that their fond memories will be spoiled if they admit their links to empire. Or perhaps their ancestors were the colonized or enslaved and the present-day person feels furious on their behalf, so furious that they can't even bring themselves to talk about it, or feel they don't know enough about empire to be able to talk about it properly. Or perhaps they just worry that the sometimes violent facts of the British Empire will be too upsetting for children.

Racism and discrimination

Another thing that stirs up strong emotions about the British Empire is the fact that racial discrimination was a key part of it. Sadly many people feel that they still suffer from racism today.

Racism was a defining feature of empire, and it involved treating people differently (and unfairly) purely because of their skin colour.

At the height of the empire, for example, there was widespread disapproval among Britons of white people having romantic relationships with non-white people. Non-white people were not generally encouraged to socialize with what imperialists considered to be their white masters. In addition, the colonized were not allowed to do a whole bunch of prestigious jobs; Lord Curzon, a man once in charge of India for the British, once made the very offensive and racist claim that 'there were no Indian natives in the government of

India because among all the 300 million people of the subcontinent, there was not a single man capable of the job'. The colonized sometimes even faced physical abuse because of their skin colour; some Indian hotels in the nineteenth century even put up notices stating 'Gentlemen are earnestly requested not to strike the servants'. Immigrants from empire found themselves facing the same racist attitudes when they moved to Britain, and some non-white people are still discriminated against today in similar ways. This is another reason why there is so much anger and pain when discussing the British Empire today.

On top of all this, the British Empire is also a very complicated subject, so it's much easier to think and talk about almost anything else instead, perhaps even dead guinea pigs and *Trollhunters*. What is certain is that whenever empire gets discussed, people get really, really upset, and when feelings run high arguments become polarized. This means that people take opposing positions, like they're football players in a game between famous rivals Manchester City and Manchester United or in a game between Wolverhampton Wanderers and West Bromwich

Albion. In these arguments the people who are 'pro' empire (meaning they support it) say things like:

The British Empire not only brought power and wealth to Britain, but it also helped the countries it colonized too. It did this by educating the "natives" (a sometimes offensive way of referring to people who were born in colonized countries) in the ways of the West, by giving them fair laws and a free press, by building railways and other infrastructure, by introducing education, and by teaching them things they didn't know. Also, by trading with them, we made the local people wealthier too. Many of the colonized people were happy the British were there looking after them. We should be proud of our great empire! And if you're not, then you're anti-British!

The people who are 'anti' empire (meaning they oppose it) might say things like:

What right did Britain ever have to just take over other countries and treat the indigenous people so brutally? We were violent and murdered them! We also killed them by exposing them to new diseases (imperialists often brought illness with them – illnesses that the indigenous peoples of Asia, Africa and Australasia hadn't developed immunity to). And sometimes Britain enslaved them. We destroyed natural resources (wrecking entire forests of mahogany, for instance, to make furniture). We hunted animals to the point of extinction. And we stole priceless artefacts for our museums. We were racist and believed the white people were the superior ruling class. And, in fact, all those railways in India were actually built to help British trade and make Britain even richer!

There are signs that the number of people who feel positive about the empire is shrinking. A survey carried out in 2016 found that 44 per cent of Britons thought that their country's 'history of colonialism' was something to be proud of, while a more recent survey showed it was lower and had dropped to around 30 per cent. But I think that viewing the British Empire through the idea of pride or shame is not useful. The problem with these pro-empire and anti-empire arguments is that there is no middle ground, no space to say 'it's complicated' or 'I'm not sure'. This kind of division also means that schools find it easier to avoid the subject entirely and just decide to teach the history of the Tudors or the Hundred Years War again and again instead.

British imperial history was long and complex. Lots of good and lots of bad things happened.

What we need to do is to try to understand what occurred and think about how that shaped us and continues to impact us today. What we don't need to do is come to a final conclusion about whether the British Empire was good or bad, as if British imperialism were a Spider-Man movie being rated on Amazon.

CURRY, DUNGAREES AND ZOMBIES

*Returning to the **bungalow** through the **jungle**, she threw her **calico** bonnet on to the **teak** table, put on her **gingham** apron and slipped into a pair of **sandals**. There was the **tea caddy** to fill, the **chutney** to prepare for the **curry**, **pepper** and **cheroots** to order from the **bazaar** – she would give the boy a **chit**. The children were out in the **dinghy** and their **khaki dungarees** were sure to be wet. She needed a **shampoo**, she still had to mend Tom's **pyjamas**, and she never had finished those **chintz** hangings for the **veranda**. Ah well! She didn't really give a **dam**, and, putting a **shawl** round her shoulders, she poured herself a **punch**.*

Don't worry, I've not totally lost the plot and started writing a novel in the middle of this history book. The above paragraph was written by historian and writer Jan Morris, who wanted to show how many words in the English language originally came from India*. True, some of these words are

---

*Jan Morris, the Pax Brittanica Trilogy, Faber & Faber, 2012.

quite old-fashioned and not used much any more. In case you're interested: *calico* is a type of cotton; *cheroots* are strong little cigars that look like twigs but taste far worse; a *chit*'s a note; and *chintz* is a type of fussy-patterned fabric that people used a lot in the days before IKEA existed. But I bet you use many of the others all the time.

Here's another important-sounding term for when you want to impress people: **etymology**. It means the origin and meaning of words. By tracing a word's history, you can learn all sorts of things about what Britain was up to at the time. They are like clues in a detective story. And it's not just words derived from India that have become part of our language. According to the *Oxford English Dictionary*, there are hundreds of other words we use that come from around the imperial world:

- **Zombie:** originally a West African word, meaning 'a soulless corpse said to have been revived by witchcraft'. Spooky!

- **Cooee:** a greeting I remember elderly neighbours using when they popped over to my childhood home. It always felt old-fashioned, but it turns out to be even older than I realized. It actually comes from the indigenous people of Australia, who the British confronted, often violently, when they colonized that part of the world in the eighteenth and nineteenth centuries. Apparently, Aboriginal Australians greeted one another with the word and the colonists copied their behaviour, using it as an alternative to 'hello'.

- **Toboggan:** originally a Native American word, meaning 'a light sledge that curves upwards and backwards at the front'. This word came into the English language when the British invaded the American homelands belonging to indigenous people.

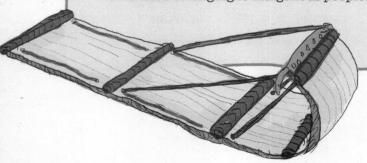

TEA

What could be more British than a cup of tea? But did you know that the hot drink that grown-ups in this country love so much does not actually come from Britain, but from distant lands? And, yes, that includes the brand that goes about calling itself Yorkshire Tea!

You may have guessed this by now, but the reason it's so widespread and popular is because of the empire. Britain first got the taste for tea during the 1600s, when sea explorers introduced the drink to Europe. Back then, all Britain's tea came from China and, although there was lots of it there, it was very rare and expensive in Britain. In fact, you might still hear people use the expression 'for all the tea in China', which you could use in a sentence such as: 'I won't do my homework for all the tea in China!' It's a way of saying that not even the gift of a large amount of a very valuable product could persuade you to do something. (Although I wouldn't recommend trying that at school - as impressed as your teachers might be with your knowledge of the history of this phrase, I don't think it'll get you out of doing your homework.)

For a while the East India Company (first discussed on page 24) dominated the international tea trade. Then in the mid-nineteenth century the situation changed. The Americans and Dutch started dabbling in the tea business too, and the Chinese threatened to cut off British supplies. The directors of the East India Company saw that 'Indian' tea would give them more control and provide a new way of making money from their growing Indian empire. So the company hired a man, Robert Fortune, to go over to China, smuggle out some tea plants and transport them to India.

This was a tricky business. As you might know yourself, it's hard enough keeping plants alive on window sills indoors, let alone when they're a load of delicate, valuable seedlings travelling in extreme weather conditions on a ship for thousands of miles. What made it even trickier was that Europeans weren't always welcome in China. So Fortune decided that the mission required a disguise, and he roamed the country wearing local clothing, dressed as a rich Chinese merchant. He shaved the front of his head and had extensions sewn into the hair on the back of his head, so it looked like he had a long ponytail. Travelling from plantation to plantation, he learned from Chinese experts how tea was processed as he collected different types of tea plants and sent them off to India.

Fortunately for Fortune (sorry, I couldn't help it) most of the plants survived in their new climate and these formed part of the basis of a major tea industry in the Darjeeling district of India. But the funny thing is that, after all that trouble, it turned out that India already had its own tea plants growing in regions such as Assam. Unsurprisingly, it was these native Indian tea plants that were the main reason for the massive growth in Indian tea production in the nineteenth century. In the end, it was the knowledge and expertise that Robert Fortune gained about tea manufacturing from China that was more important than any plants he managed to smuggle into India. It sounds like it should be a proverb, doesn't it? Sometimes the tea you're looking for in foreign lands is actually at your feet all along!

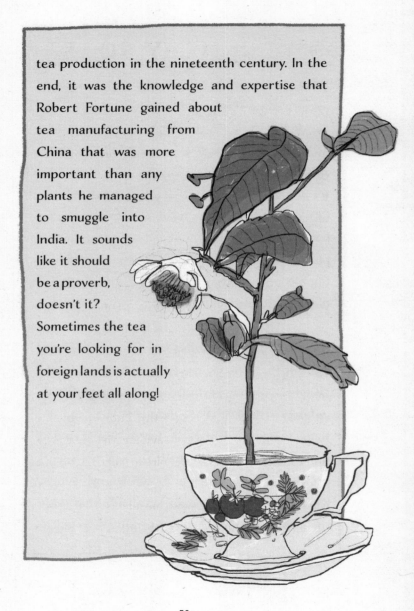

THE SUNDAY ROAST

What is Britain's national dish? People usually answer this question with either fish and chips, or chicken tikka masala, or a Sunday roast. Here's another question: which of these three national dishes is not connected to the British Empire? It's a trick question, because you could argue they all are.

How fish and chips became such a classic pairing is unknown – before battered fish was introduced to Britain, it was made by Sephardic people (Spanish or Portuguese Jews) on a weekly basis – but cod fishermen knew something that became invaluable to British colonizers. These fishermen played an important role in learning how to sail boats on the Atlantic Ocean, and it was this knowledge that helped imperial explorers navigate the same sea and establish the British Empire in North America.

Meanwhile, chicken tikka masala is a product of our long relationship with India, and it was introduced by immigrants (people who left their homeland to live in a foreign country) from the subcontinent. If you want to know more about the man who established the first curry house in Britain, then turn to the section on shampoo on page 159 (I know this sounds odd, but I promise it will make sense soon!).

And how is a Sunday roast linked to the British Empire? Well, British people have always really liked meat. In fact, the French still sometimes refer to the English by the nickname *les rosbifs*, which means 'the roast beefs'. But up until the nineteenth century meat was expensive and only eaten regularly by the rich; poorer people might have had roast meat only on very special occasions, like Christmas. In an attempt to make meat cheaper, the British tried to ship live animals over from America. But this didn't work as the animals got stressed by the journey and were often injured or died as a result. Then, in 1875, a farmer found a way of transporting meat rather than live cattle by using a special refrigerated boat. This worked, and tons of meat were brought into Britain, which the country was very happy about. But by this stage the USA had broken free of the British Empire, and Britain thought it would be better if the meat came from its colonies in Australia and New Zealand. Then Britain would be in control of the trade and it could be thought of as 'British meat'.

The only problem was that Australia and New Zealand were much further away than America – the meat would have to travel 13,000 nautical miles through the Tropics! A floating fridge wouldn't be enough – this job needed a floating freezer, which would be colder and preserve the meat better. Some very clever people got to work and invented technology that made it possible to send frozen meat from one side of the world to the other. Once thawed out, the meat was tasty, and, despite all the travel involved, it was cheaper than meat from America or, sometimes, even meat from animals raised in Britain.

This technology made meat cheap and plentiful enough for everyone in Britain – not just the wealthy – to enjoy a roast every week. By the 1890s Britain alone consumed a whopping 60 per cent of all the meat that was traded around the world, which was largely possible because of its empire. Pretty a-moo-zing!

CHAPTER 3

Is all the stuff in our museums nicked?

Well, not all of it. But some of the imperial exhibits are. Before we go on, though, the phrase we're going to use here is not 'nicked' or 'stolen' or 'snaffled' or 'pinched' but 'looted', because this word specifically means taking things by force. And unfortunately that's the story behind many of the colonial artefacts in British museums. It's also another English word that actually comes from India – it derives from *lut*, the Hindi word for spoils of war – and it feels right that we use a stolen word to describe such theft.

In Victorian times, when the empire was at its peak, it was a popular hobby among the men who went out into the colonies to collect rare and interesting objects. Sometimes they would take objects that were obviously valuable, such as diamonds. Other times, what they were interested in were things that they saw as exotic and intriguing, including animals such as monkeys, leopards and Indian rhino (see page 75).

Some imperialists and soldiers saw looting as a perk of the job, and treated it as the nineteenth-century version of bringing back a fridge magnet or T-shirt from a foreign holiday. Sometimes the things taken were looted on behalf of the nation and given to the royal family. Some of the looted objects stayed with the families of the individuals who took them and were later donated or sold to museums. Sometimes museums' representatives were present as the looting happened and took a share.

There were various reasons why the British took things that didn't belong to them:

1. **Plain old greed.**
2. **Curiosity.**

Some of the objects taken were extremely valuable. One example is the Maqdala Crown. This golden crown is an amazing work of craftsmanship commissioned by the Ethiopian Empress Mentewab in the 1740s. It was looted when the British invaded Ethiopia in 1868. William Gladstone was prime minister at the time, and he was very shocked when he heard this crown and other artefacts had been looted. He told the House of Commons that he felt incredibly sad that these items 'were thought fit to be brought away by a British army'. He urged that they 'be held only until they could be restored' – given back. Yet the crown has been on display at the Victoria and Albert Museum (V&A) in London for more than 150 years.

In 1903, Britain invaded Tibet. The British killed up to 3,000 Tibetans and looted a load of rare religious artefacts, books and manuscripts. This was mainly because Britain wanted to know more about the country. Since 1792 Tibet had blocked Europeans from entering, and only one Englishman had managed to enter its capital, Lhasa. As one of the last unmapped spots on the planet, Tibet was the ultimate goal for explorers. In many ways the mysteriousness of Tibet was a little like modern-day North Korea – a country that does not allow many visitors from the West.

Another looted artefact that we still have today is called Tipu's Tiger. This is a large wooden mechanical figure of a European soldier lying on his back, being mauled by a tiger, and it has been on show at the V&A for centuries. It previously belonged to Tipu Sultan, the once feared ruler of a city named Mysore in India, but it came into British hands in 1799 after he was defeated and killed by – you've guessed it – the East India Company. Tipu Sultan might have ordered

the mechanical toy to be built because it showed his enemy being defeated, but when it was put on display in London British people once again showed their curiosity, flocking to it because they thought it demonstrated how cruel some Indian rulers could be.

The looting of artefacts was often very disorganized.

When the British invaded and looted the city of Benin in what is now Nigeria in 1897, thousands of objects were taken. You can see some of them on display in the British Museum. Sometimes the things taken by colonialists were human body parts: the teeth and heads of defeated enemies, for example. Understandably, many people from former colonies still feel deeply upset that their ancestors might be stored in this way and were never given proper funerals.

Lots of other items looted during the empire had religious or spiritual importance and were very precious to the people they were taken from. When I

think of everything that was looted by the British, it is not the heaps of gold, jewellery, antiques, textiles, paintings and sculptures that hurts for me, as a Sikh. The looting that really hurts involved the British taking religious artefacts from the Sikh Empire in India. This empire was established by Maharajah Ranjit Singh, and it existed in northern India from 1799 to 1849, when it was defeated and conquered by the English. The British took ownership at this point of the famous Koh-i-Noor diamond (see page 69), and also rare religious artefacts; these were said to include relics of the Prophet Muhammad, the founder of the Muslim religion, Islam, and Guru Gobind Singh's *kalgi*, a jewel worn on the front of a turban by one of the founders of my religion. Heartbreakingly, both items then went missing.

Sometimes even pets weren't safe. When the British invaded China and burned China's Summer Palace in 1860, officers came across a Pekinese dog and decided to take it back home as a gift for Queen Victoria.

Believe it or not, they named the dog . . . Looty.

All this might give the impression that looting was acceptable at the time, but it wasn't always. The British public, British politicians and sometimes even members of the royal family disapproved. But even after inter-national laws had been introduced to ban such behaviour, looting continued. British soldiers would often say that they had purchased the objects fairly or had been given them by locals. Sometimes this was true – there were some honest people working for the British Empire, and unique friendships did form between the colonizers and the colonized. But quite often such claims of 'fair deals' deliberately didn't tell the full story.

Imagine, for example, that there's someone at school who you're scared of. This person might be cruel to people (or hang out with a mean crowd) and be known to lose their temper. Now imagine that person asks you to sell them your PS5, your pet rabbit or your most treasured Pokémon card for the small price of fifty pence. You might feel pressured to give them what they want, even if they aren't actually threatening or hurting you. So, yes, they might claim that they had bought your treasured object in a 'fair deal', but it wasn't actually fair at all, was it? This kind of thing sometimes happened during the empire. At other times British soldiers would promise to give locals something in return for their precious items – but then simply broke their promise.

Returning loot

Now that the empire is long over and we are learning more about the unfair and often violent ways that Britain came to possess these looted objects, you won't be surprised to hear that many people in the former colonies would like their things back. But Britain is reluctant to return them. Why? That's a good question! But you won't be surprised to hear that the answer isn't simple.

First, you need to know the word 'repatriation'. This means the process of returning something to its own country. Repatriation is a very hot issue in Britain and in the other former imperial powers of Europe, such as France and Germany. When French President Emmanuel Macron came to power in 2017, he declared that he would repatriate anything his country had taken from its African colonies. But, on the whole, Britain hasn't been quite so keen. Some of our smaller museums, such as Manchester Museum, and universities and private collectors, have repatriated objects taken during the empire. But our larger national museums, which are home to the most famous disputed objects, are more reluctant. There are a few reasons that they give for this:

1. **It's not easy.**

   It's a long, tricky process to investigate which objects were looted, and which were bought or given fairly.

2. **Who gets what?**

   Hundreds of years after the looting was done, sometimes it's not clear who you'd return the items to.

3. **Value to the museum.**

   Many of these objects are popular attractions in our museums, and to lose them would be a blow.

4. **Drawing the line.**

   There's a worry that if museums return one thing, they'll have to return lots of others. In 2010, India asked for the return of the Koh-i-Noor diamond (see page 69). Prime Minister David Cameron argued, 'If you say yes to one, you suddenly find the British Museum would be empty . . . It is going to have to stay put.'

I feel this is misleading. The British Museum only has about 1 per cent of its collection on display, and even if every controversial item being requested back was returned overnight, I suspect it would still have most of its collection.

In the light of this disagreement, you might feel concerned about visiting museums. You shouldn't. They are generally staffed by people who want to talk about these issues, and there will be suggestions later in this book about how you might engage with them. There are also small signs that our big museums are finally responding to pressure. Some of them are making efforts to loan disputed items back to the original owners on a long-term basis. A former government minister in charge of Britain's biggest museums has said that more items should be repatriated. Some museums have also put up signs beside looted objects explaining their history and the unfair ways they came to Britain.

You might feel that this is not going far enough or progressing quickly enough, but it's a start.

A CROWN JEWEL

If you've ever been to see the Crown Jewels – the British royal family's collection of valuable items worn by kings and queens throughout history – at the Tower of London, you'll know there's much to be dazzled by. The collection includes over 23,000 gemstones spread over more than a hundred priceless objects. That's a whole lot of bling! So much bling that you may not notice one particular diamond that sits in a crown once worn by the mother of Queen Elizabeth II, the grandmother of King Charles III – although it really is massive, and quite hard to miss. This diamond is the Koh-i-Noor (also spelled Koh-i-Nûr or Kohinoor), which means 'Mountain of Light' in Persian. The diamond has a long and dramatic history, ever since it was found in India many hundreds of years ago, and some people believe it doesn't belong in Britain at all.

The diamond has had many owners, including the Mughals who ruled India for centuries before the British arrived. They used the gem to adorn their emperor's famous Peacock Throne. In 1813, the Koh-i-Noor became the property of the founder of the Sikh Empire, Maharajah Ranjit Singh (see page 63). The gem was his most prized possession – aside from it being worth a lot of money, he felt it had an almost supernatural power. One writer describes it as being a bit like the ring in *The Lord of the Rings*, which symbolizes evil and obsesses those who pursue it. But the Koh-i-Noor also caught the eye of the East India Company, which by this time was calling the shots in India. In 1849, Ranjit Singh died, and the throne – and diamond – was passed to his son, a ten-year boy called Duleep Singh.

The British took this as their chance to nab the diamond. When the British invaded the Sikh kingdom of the Punjab, they imprisoned the boy's mother and forced the child to sign a document that passed the diamond to the British and gave up his claim to the throne. Duleep Singh became the last maharajah of the Sikh Empire and ended up in the care of Dr John Login, a Scottish surgeon working in British India. Singh was brought up like a British boy, given British children's books and encouraged to read the Bible. He learned so much about Christianity that he eventually abandoned his Sikh faith and converted.

The East India Company brought the diamond to England and presented it to Queen Victoria in 1850. It was put on display, but the public were disappointed and felt that it wasn't shiny enough! So the royals had it cut down and polished to look even more impressive. It was then worn as a brooch by Queen Victoria, before it made its way into the Crown Jewels.

With so many of its owners living lives filled with violence, murder and treachery, it's perhaps not surprising that some people believe that the Koh-i-Noor is cursed! The superstition that it curses men is the reason why only British queens, not kings, have worn it. Nonetheless, there's a campaign for the Koh-i-Noor to be returned to India, with many arguing that it should be given back to the country where it was originally found. But for now it's staying put under armed guard at the Tower of London. Do you dare go and see it?

LONDON ZOO

If you've ever been to a zoo, you'll know the number-one rule: don't feed the animals! Back in 1831, however, things were different. When an Indian elephant called Jack arrived at London Zoo, a stall was set up beside his enclosure selling cakes and buns, so people could enjoy watching Jack pick up the baked goods and gobble them down.

You might think this was a welcome treat for Jack, especially as he had endured a nine-month-long sea voyage from Madras in India via China to get to his new home. Like many of the animals that filled the zoo in its early years, he came from one of Britain's colonies. The empire gave Britain access to many creatures that weren't usually found on its island nation, and this was one of the things that led to London Zoo being created in 1828.

The zoo is part of the Zoological Society of London, which was set up by a man called Sir Thomas Stamford Raffles, an East India Company officer who is also famous for having founded Singapore, the island colony which is also a country. Raffles had previously lived in India, where baby tiger cubs roamed freely around his house and a monkey entertained guests at dinner. When he came back to London, he decided to set up a society to study animals and natural history. Previously, wild animals in Britain had not been treated very well. They were kept in cramped, miserable conditions, including in the Tower of London, but Raffles wanted to create a large open space for the animals instead, where people could observe them leading relatively natural lives, as they would in the wild. Regent's Park in London was chosen as the spot. Unfortunately Raffles died before seeing his zoo built, but others took over his mission.

Jack

Soon exotic animals from all over the empire began arriving at the zoo, including an Indian rhino bought for what would now be around £145,000. There were also monkeys, leopards, bears, kangaroos and, most excitingly, a camelopard. A what?! A camelopard is what people used to call giraffes – because they thought they looked like a cross between a camel and a leopard!

Sadly, many of these precious animals didn't survive long. They had been plucked from their natural hot habitats and had gone through long, traumatic sea journeys to end up in a cold disease-ridden city (lots of horrible illnesses affecting humans and animals at the time didn't have cures, treatments or vaccinations). And also, as shown by Jack's never-ending bun feast, the people at the zoo didn't really know how to look after them properly. Fortunately animal welfare has improved a lot since then and London Zoo does loads of good conservation work to protect wildlife. But not all progress is good. 'Giraffe' is a boring name – let's bring back the camelopard!

CRICKET

Cricket was the sport of the British Empire. Of course, other games were played across the colonies, like rugby and football, and chess and cards when people were feeling lazy, but the favourite by far was cricket. You might think this is odd, because football is the most popular sport around the world today. Football needs less equipment than cricket, and the rules are much easier to understand. So surely it makes more sense for football to be the game that the British Empire spread across the planet?

As it happens, the British Empire did play a big role in spreading football round the world, but cricket was favoured by imperialists because it was the most popular sport in British public schools, and, at the height of the empire in Victorian times, pretty much all the people who ran the empire were men who had gone to public schools. (Public schools are schools that only accept certain students, and which usually cost a lot of money to attend. So 'public school' is a silly name, as most of the public can't and won't be able to go to them! Some people prefer to call them 'private schools', because they are funded by private individuals, which I think makes more sense.) When these men went abroad to the colonies, they took cricket with them. The British colonizers liked playing it because it reminded them of home. They also feared that a hot climate was bad for their health, and playing cricket felt like a way of keeping fit and healthy. In the nineteenth century the Imperial Cricket Conference (the governing body for world cricket, which was founded by representatives from Australia, England and South Africa, and now goes by the name of the International Cricket Conference) created a universal set of rules for the game. This meant that it could be played in the same way in every country across the empire.

But cricket was seen as more than just a sport; it represented the values that the British wanted to spread around the world. They insisted that cricket was about courage, resilience, teamwork and, above all, fair play. And they claimed that those values were what the empire was all about – although, of course, many people would disagree with this.

Because the British thought that playing cricket helped to build good character, they encouraged the people they colonized to play it too. And soon the local people in the colonies learned to beat the British at their own game (in more ways than one). Today all the leading international cricket sides, such as India, Pakistan, Australia and Sri Lanka, are former British colonies. And the game is still used as a measure of good behaviour. If something unfair has just happened, you might hear someone say 'But that's just not cricket!'

CHAPTER 4

How did the British Empire
shape our towns, cities
and countryside?

Stately homes are everywhere in Britain. They're the enormous buildings that are, or used to be, the homes of incredibly wealthy, usually posh families. You might live quite close to one. You may well have visited one for a school trip or on a day out with your family. You might have seen one on TV too – in a period drama such as *Downton Abbey* or *Pride and Prejudice*, or in films about Harry Potter or James Bond.

The biggest ones are truly jaw-dropping, such as Powis Castle in Wales or Harewood House in Yorkshire, which has so many rooms that staff spend two and a half hours a week just changing light bulbs. Even the smaller ones are seriously grand, with antiques everywhere and sweeping manicured gardens usually complete with a herd of deer, roaming peacocks and a ha-ha (yes, 'ha-ha' is a real word! It's a ditch used by owners who don't want their views interrupted by a wall or fence. It stops grazing animals from wandering into places where they're not wanted and its name comes from the way it surprised people who hadn't noticed it from a distance, making them cry 'Ha! Ha!').

There's usually a nice cafe where everything costs too much – but then many of these stately homes are incredibly expensive to run. Those light bulbs won't pay for themselves! Often they are now managed by charities such as the National Trust and English Heritage, but between the mid-sixteenth and mid-nineteenth centuries, they were sometimes private houses for people with colonial wealth. In other words, they were owned by families who had made money from plantations in the Caribbean where enslaved people worked or from trading with (and often exploiting) India. ('To exploit' means to take advantage of someone or something.)

A man (and it was almost always a man) could acquire a stately home like this in lots of different ways. For example:

1. They could marry into a family that was already rich with colonial wealth.

2. They could go to work for the East India Company, a job that was seen then as a way of getting rich quick but often exposed these men to a hot climate and dangerous diseases such as yellow fever (a virus spread by infected mosquitoes) that they might die from.

3. They could own and run a West Indian plantation, where they would use enslaved workers to produce sugar, cotton, rum and/or coffee. Although they were also likely to get sick here.

4. Or they could be merchants, trading goods for captured African people who they then transported to plantations in the West Indies and America.

The type of slavery used on these plantations was 'chattel slavery'. Under this system, the enslaved, and their children, were the property of their owners for life – they could be forced to do any kind of work, at any time, and could be bought or sold at any time like jewellery or furniture. Slave plantations were places where extreme violence was common: such cruelty was often thought to be the only way to get the enslaved to work so hard, often leading to their death. They received no payment for producing crops like sugar, cotton and tobacco and were forced to live in appalling conditions. This made slave plantations cheap to run and often made the owners extremely rich.

Not everyone who profited from the slave trade played an active role in it. Many people stayed in Britain and invested their money in it, as if it was any old business opportunity, like buying shares in a company like Tesla or Disney nowadays.

The slave trade even had the royal seal of approval. Back in the 1660s, Charles II and his brother, the Duke of York (later James II), helped to found the Royal African Company, which shipped more enslaved

African people to the Americas than any other company in the history of the Atlantic slave trade. When the enslaved arrived in places like Barbados, some had the initials for the Duke of York ('DY') branded, or burned, into their skin. Because of horrific practices such as this, and because of the overall cruelty of the slave trade, even when it was legal, many British people were disgusted and angered by it. The anger was so intense that some of those who made money from it acted as if their wealth had come from somewhere else. But the fact remains that a lot of people were involved and made their wealth from the slave trade in some way. In 1833, when slavery was abolished across the British Empire, it was estimated there were 46,000 owners of enslaved people in Britain.

Stately homes are not the only legacies that remain from the empire (a legacy is something that comes from the past). There are legacies that are still around today in the form of buildings, ports, bridges, institutions, street names and statues. Let's go on a journey through Britain and look at the many ways in which the British Empire shaped the nation.

London

We'll start our trip in London, the capital city of England. London is famous as a world financial centre. This reputation was earned during the empire, when lots of British banks made a great deal of money by loaning it to people who were trading in India or running businesses in the Caribbean, which relied on the work of enslaved people.

Some of the companies that made money from the slave trade still operate today. They include many of the country's biggest banks, law firms and some international accountancy firms. For example, William Welch Deloitte, the founder of a large accounting company called Deloitte, was the grandson of a West Indies planter (someone who made money from running plantations in the West Indies).

There are also several grand government offices in London that exist because of the empire. For example, the building now called the Foreign, Commonwealth and Development Office was built at the height of the empire for imperial officials. Inside, the offices are full of paintings and statues of famous imperialists, and art celebrating the British Empire.

You can find many imperial figures standing, proudly displayed in stone and bronze, all over the country, but many are in London – so let's go on a whistlestop tour and see what they tell us about the British Empire.

SIR WALTER RALEIGH

1552–1618

Statue located at Old Royal Naval
College, Greenwich, London

The Elizabethan explorer Sir Walter Raleigh is best known for introducing two important things to Britain and Ireland. One is the potato (yay, chips!). The other is tobacco (boo, cigarettes!). He is also famous for supposedly laying his cloak over a puddle to protect the feet of the queen, Elizabeth I. No wonder he was one of her favourites in court!

In the sixteenth century, when the Spanish were colonizing parts of the Americas, Raleigh thought England needed to compete and develop similar colonies. With the Queen's blessing, he organized a sea expedition that eventually led to the founding of the first English colony in North America on what was then called Roanoke Island; he named it Virginia. But his attempt to colonize North America was unsuccessful and the colony was short-lived.

He also led a mission to find a lost ancient city full of riches called El Dorado in South America, which failed, mainly because El Dorado does not exist! The term 'El Dorado' has stayed in our language, however, to mean a city or country rich in gold.

The monarch who came after Elizabeth, James I, didn't like Raleigh and imprisoned him in the Tower of London. James eventually let him out to go on another mission to find El Dorado, but when Raleigh returned empty-handed, and was discovered to have disobeyed certain orders, he was sentenced to death. In 1618, he had his head chopped off outside the Palace of Westminster. Life could be harsh in those days! It puts my school cross-country runs into perspective anyway.

Raleigh's statue was erected in 1959, to commemorate the 350th anniversary of the founding of the colony of Virginia. The statue was originally sited in Whitehall in central London, but it was moved because it was too small and looked ridiculous compared to the other statues around it. Oh dear, Elizabeth I's favourite explorer would not have liked that at all. Then again, he had bigger problems.

ROBERT CLIVE

1725–1774

Statue located in King Charles Street,
Whitehall, London

If there's one Brit who could claim to have founded the British Empire in India, or at least got it going, it would have to be Robert Clive. He was the man who led the East India Company's army, and won several important battles including the Battle of Plassey in 1757, which gave the British control over the region. This success led to Clive becoming the Governor of Bengal, which was a very powerful position, with lots of perks. As governor, he made poor people pay very high taxes they couldn't afford, which led to a terrible famine in 1770 that killed millions.

Back in England, Clive enjoyed the fruits of his time in India – namely lots and lots and LOTS of cash. If his own estimates were correct, he made the modern equivalent of around £700 million. Jaw-dropping! He spent this money on multiple grand stately homes, and, if newspaper reports are to be believed, on a diamond necklace for his wife's pet ferret. I hope you pamper your pets in similar style!

For someone who got so much out of India, Clive didn't seem to like it much. He described Indians as lazy, ignorant and cowardly, and claimed that at the end of his first year there he had 'not enjoyed one happy day'. Because of Clive's behaviour in India, there have been calls for his statues around Britain to be taken down. Even his direct descendant, John Herbert, the eighth Earl of Powis, has said he is uncomfortable with his ancestor's statue in his home town of Shrewsbury and would like it removed. For now, though, his statue stands in London, its inscription simply reading 'CLIVE'. He was a man so famous – or infamous (which means terrible or monstrous) – that he only needed one name.

PRINCE ALBERT
1819–1861

Statue located in
Kensington Gardens, London

The massive Albert Memorial in London's Kensington Gardens, which resembles a rocket on a launchpad (if Victorians had rockets and launchpads, and if rockets could be made of stone), is just one of many memorials and statues dedicated to Prince Albert around the country. There's also a statue of him on horseback in nearby Holborn Circus, as well as tributes to him in Aberdeen, Belfast, Edinburgh, Liverpool and Wolverhampton. Oh, and let's not forget his name is used for the Royal Albert Hall and the Victoria and Albert Museum.

The sheer number of statues reflect how much Queen Victoria adored her husband. They were cousins and married when they were both twenty. As was usually the case with royal marriages, the match was set up by others, but Victoria and Albert also truly loved each other. We know this through letters and accounts of the time. Victoria wrote things about Albert like: 'His excessive love and affection gave me feelings of heavenly love and happiness.' Cute. They also ended up having nine children!

Before Albert died at the age of forty-two (that's young,

by the way!), he fought for the abolition (ending) of slavery. In the same year he married Victoria, he gave his first public speech in Britain at the meeting of the Society for the Abolition of Slavery.

In the speech he described slavery as 'the desolation of Africa and the blackest stain upon civilized Europe'.

Slavery had actually been formally abolished across the British Empire in 1833, seven years before this speech, so Albert was talking about the slavery that remained elsewhere. There is some question whether such a speech would have been made fifty years earlier, before British slavery had been abolished and when the country was profiting hugely from the slave trade. After all, his role was to support the royal family, and the British monarchy had a long history of involvement in the slave trade.

Albert wasn't against the British Empire as a whole. Quite the opposite, he thought it was a marvellous thing – which is fortunate as his wife would one day be given the title of Empress of India! Still, Albert's public condemnation of worldwide slavery reminds us that Britain did eventually make efforts to stamp out slavery across the planet. He also spoke out against child labour and deserves recognition for this. Although perhaps not with quite so many statues!

MARY SEACOLE
1805–1881

Statue located at
St Thomas' Hospital, London

The Crimean War was a conflict between Russia, Britain and Britain's allies, which took place between 1853 and 1856, mainly on the Crimean Peninsula in what is now Ukraine. Mary Seacole was born in the British colony of Jamaica to a Jamaican mother and Scottish father, and she trained as a nurse. When the Crimean War started, she travelled to England and tried to enlist as an army nurse to help the war effort. The authorities rejected her, which Mary could only assume was because of the colour of her skin and the intense racism of the time. But Mary was determined. She travelled to the Crimea anyway and set up a refuge and restaurant for sick and wounded soldiers. She even rode on horseback on to the battlefield itself to tend to the wounded – both those on the British side and the Russian.

Another nurse had also travelled out to the Crimea to help the soldiers, and her name was Florence Nightingale. Both nurses were celebrated for their kindness, bravery and dedication. Mary also wrote a bestselling book about her time in the Crimea, which was one of the first travel books ever published by a Black woman. But, after Mary's death in 1881, like so many once prominent people of colour who achieved great things, Mary faded from history, while Florence Nightingale – 'The Lady with the Lamp', and a white woman – remained a household name.

A century later, Mary's achievements were 'rediscovered', and people campaigned for her to get the recognition she deserved. Mary's bronze statue, which was unveiled in 2016, is nearly five metres tall, and depicts her striding purposefully forward carrying a medicine bag. The sculptor said he wanted to show her 'confronting head-on some of the personal resistance she had constantly to battle', such as racial prejudice. It's thought to be the first memorial statue of a named Black woman (rather than a symbolic figure) in Britain.

MAHATMA GANDHI
1869–1948

Statue located in
Parliament Square, London

Right outside the Houses of Parliament you can find a collection of A-list statues. To get remembered here it helps to have been a prime minister. But since 2015 figures such as Winston Churchill and Benjamin Disraeli have been joined by Mahatma Gandhi, who was not a prime minister. In fact, he dedicated a large amount of his life to fighting Britain, rather than representing it like the others. His inclusion in the square shows his importance – he changed the destiny of the British Empire.

Gandhi was the leader of the movement to end British rule in India. He engaged in non-violent protest to achieve this and was ultimately successful, with India becoming independent in 1947. As India was by far the largest and most important colony for the British, when the country broke away it signalled the beginning of the end of the British Empire. So, considering Gandhi was against the empire and could be held responsible for its end, it might seem a bit strange that he's celebrated in Parliament Square! Indeed, the British prime minister for some of the time Gandhi protested was Winston Churchill, whose statue stands nearby.

Churchill was against Indian independence and really didn't like Gandhi. However, Britain's attitude towards India changed after the Second World War. Churchill and his Conservative government were voted out, a new Labour government came in, and the country didn't have the money or energy to govern colonies the way it used to. At midnight on 14 August 1947, India became free from Britain. Most people in Britain realized that letting India go was the right thing to do, and eventually Gandhi became recognized as a hero.

Indian independence was a painful process, which included dividing the country up into two broadly Hindu and Muslim nations, India and Pakistan, with about 15 million people moving or being forced to move.

This process, called Partition, caused massive conflict between the groups – between 1 and 2 million people died in the violence that followed, and tensions remain to this day.

In his statue Gandhi is dressed in the humble outfit he became famous for wearing: a loincloth and sandals. The plinth the statue stands on is lower than the others on the square, which was done on purpose to show that Gandhi saw himself as a man of the people, at their level rather than above them.

MAJOR-GENERAL
CHARLES GORDON
1833–1885

Statue located in Victoria Embankment
Gardens, London

Weekly magazines were very popular with boys growing up in late-Victorian times. They had titles like *The Boy's Own Paper*, and were filled with patriotic adventure stories, often with an imperial theme. They frequently contained pictures of the empire's heroes for children to put on their bedroom walls. And one of the figures they were most obsessed with, the Harry Kane of the imperial world, was Major-General Charles Gordon. He was so important that he got two titles! To match what sounded like two first names! Gordon was an officer in the British army who became the Governor-General (that's yet another title) of Sudan in Africa. Sudan was then officially controlled by Egypt, but Egypt was controlled by Britain, and so Britain effectively ruled Sudan too. After some years in Sudan, Gordon came back to England, but when a revolt broke out in his former colonial territory, he was sent back there to deal with it.

The British prime minister at the time, William Gladstone, did not want Britain to get involved in the revolt, and ordered Gordon to evacuate the capital city Khartoum, which was under siege. Instead, Gordon decided to stay put in the city, in the hope of rescuing all the civilians trapped there. Gordon wrote to Gladstone asking for reinforcements, but Gladstone hesitated – after all, Gordon was disobeying his orders. Gordon and his troops managed to defend the city for almost a year until the enemy broke in and killed him. Just two days later, but two days too late, reinforcements from Britain finally arrived. Gordon's body was never found.

The British public were very upset about Gordon's death. They saw him as a true hero and he was the perfect example of how the British liked to see themselves during the empire: courageous and fighting for the greater good against those who were, in their minds, racially and morally inferior. So it's perhaps no surprise that London is littered with tributes to him. In fact, you could spend a whole day visiting them. As well as this statue, there are memorials to him in Westminster Abbey and St Paul's Cathedral, and a whopping twenty-six portraits of him in the National Portrait Gallery alone!

CHARLES IGNATIUS SANCHO
1729–1780

And here is one person who doesn't have a statue, but who I think perhaps should. The man I'm nominating was an acclaimed writer, composer and social campaigner, as well as being a shopkeeper. These would be impressive enough achievements for anyone in the eighteenth century, but they are particularly extraordinary for a Black man living in London during a time when many Africans across the British Empire were enslaved – as he once had been too. Also, Charles Ignatius Sancho can claim a number of firsts. He was the first Black person in Britain to vote. He was the first Black person in Britain to publish his music. And he was the first known Black person to have his obituary (an account of his life) printed in a newspaper when he died.

But I'm getting ahead of myself. Let's go back to the beginning. Charles was born in 1729 on a slave ship travelling from West Africa to the West Indies. He was soon an orphan – his mother died when he was tiny and his father took his own life, as he refused to spend his life enslaved. The young enslaved boy was then transported to London to work for three sisters, which was a miserable existence. However, his fortunes changed when he met a kind duke who saw his potential and helped him become educated.

When the duke died, Charles ran away from the three sisters and went to work for the duke's surviving family. From there Charles established himself in London. He married a West Indian woman and had seven children, and together they opened a food shop in central London. He composed music and wrote letters, many of which were to newspapers calling for the abolition of slavery. Because he was clever, educated and entertaining – and perhaps also because he was seen as 'exotic' – London society accepted him. He became friends with many influential people and had his portrait painted by a famous artist called Thomas Gainsborough. Alongside all his achievements and campaigning, what I admire about Charles Ignatius Sancho is his courage. It must have taken immense bravery and so much energy to achieve all that he did.

He died in 1780 and was buried in the churchyard of St Margaret's in London. There's a plaque celebrating his achievements not far from Downing Street. It announces that the:

> **Writer, symbol of the humanity of Africans, lived and had a grocery shop near this site**

It is nice, but I feel he deserves a statue at least as big as that of Clive, which stands imposingly nearby.

Can you think of any other examples of people who you believe deserve statues?

Lancashire

We're hopping on a train for a few hours to head north to Lancashire now. Here you can still see the textile mills where cotton picked by enslaved people on plantations was woven into cloth. Textile mills are factories that deal with natural fabrics, whether that's processing cotton, weaving fabric, bleaching, dyeing or printing. By the end of the nineteenth century, more than 500,000 people were working for the textile industry in Lancashire, most of them involved with the production of cotton goods. Up until the 1860s, most of the cotton used by these mills had been gathered by enslaved people in the southern states of America. In 1862, some Lancashire mill workers took a stand. They refused to touch cotton picked by enslaved people in the US. This protest led to many workers facing poverty and starvation.

The British textile industry collapsed in the twentieth century and lots of the textile mills have been lost through demolition, decay and fire. Those that survived were often converted into modern offices and homes.

Liverpool

It's only around 35 miles between Manchester (in Lancashire) and Liverpool – a journey that is about an hour in a car, about forty minutes by train and eleven and a half hours if you walk! I wouldn't recommend the last option. For a while Liverpool was the largest site for building slave ships in Britain – the boats that transported enslaved people from the continent of Africa across the seas. The city also made lots of money from slave-grown sugar and cotton. By 1740 thirty-three slave ships set sail from there each year. Liverpool ended up becoming a large and grand city – vessels from the city carried about 40 per cent of the entire Atlantic slave trade and controlled up to 60 per cent of the British trade.

These industries brought much wealth to Liverpool and many of its important buildings were constructed as a result. If you look closely at the town hall walls, you'll see they are decorated with trading routes, lions, crocodiles, elephants and African faces – all hinting at this history.

Bristol

We're now moving down to Bristol, a major slaving port in the seventeenth and eighteenth centuries. Here local merchants were responsible for transporting hundreds of thousands of enslaved people in what was called the 'triangular trade'. This involved sending goods like brass and copper rods on boats from Bristol to West Africa, where they would be traded for enslaved people. The enslaved would then be taken to plantations in the Americas, with many not surviving the journey. Finally, the boats would be loaded with sugar, tobacco and cotton to bring back to Bristol.

One of the traders in Bristol was a man called Edward Colston. He spent a lot of his profits from slavery on building schools and institutions for the poor in his community. (It seems odd, I know, that someone would make money from the suffering of some people and then spend it on improving the lives of others. But these slave traders didn't view Black human beings as equal to white human beings.)

For a long time a statue of Colston stood at Bristol docks. To many people this statue looming over the city served as a reminder of the suffering of enslaved Black people, and in 2020 it was pulled down by Black Lives Matter protestors. They felt that a slave trader should not be honoured, however much money he had given to the city. The Black Lives Matter movement was founded in 2013. Their campaigns highlight how in the current state of the world Black lives seem to matter less than other lives. Black Lives Matter is a call for Black people to be treated equally. The toppling of the statue opened up a new conversation about what should be done about such legacies of the slave trade, and this discussion continues to this day (see page 187).

Oxford

There has been a similar debate in Oxford, a city in the middle of England. This famous university town wasn't directly connected to the slave trade like Bristol, but many wealthy imperialists and slave owners gave large amounts of money to the university and are honoured there with plaques and statues. The most infamous of these is a man named Cecil Rhodes, who even had a country named after him, Rhodesia (now Zimbabwe). He was a firm believer in white supremacy (the false and dangerous belief that white people are superior to other races), and he became extremely rich while running his own colony in Africa.

He made some extraordinarily racist remarks, claiming that the Anglo-Saxon people behind the British Empire 'happen to be the best people in the world, with the highest ideals of decency and justice and liberty and peace, and the more of the world we inhabit, the better it is for humanity'. There is an ongoing argument in Oxford about whether the university should continue to honour Rhodes through memorials on public display, when he had such harmful racist beliefs.

We cannot be responsible for what British people did in the past. But it is important for us to think about the ways we do or don't honour the people, buildings and other legacies from the empire that still remain. For example, organizations such as English Heritage and the National Trust have made great efforts to look into the properties they own and to be open and honest about their links to colonial and slave histories. The National Trust recently reported that almost a third of its 300 houses and gardens were built with or supported by wealth from slavery, or contain treasures looted from overseas. While no one can change the past, it is important not to deliberately ignore this essential history and to bring it to life so people know the truth.

This might leave you wondering whether you should be visiting somewhere like a stately home if it has strong colonial links. Or maybe you're questioning what you should do if you do visit these places. If you want to learn about a particular place, you can always look at the official website and see if the history of the house is discussed there. You can also ask questions when you get there. But keep in mind that some people resist talking about this kind of history (as discussed in the last chapter) or skate over the dark facts. For instance, one history website describes the man who built Harewood House, Edwin Lascelles, simply as a trader involved in business with the West Indies. This is another example of a euphemism (see page 33). The truth is that this family became one of the richest families in Britain through the slave trade. They built their reputation and wealth on the ill-treatment, torture and murder of innocent people. In fact, they owned sugar plantations in the Caribbean until the 1970s!

Personally I would never say that it's wrong to visit anywhere because of its history. The key is to do your research, to have conversations with people and to share knowledge. As you might have started to notice by now, if you tried to avoid anything that was 'tainted' by colonialism, you wouldn't have much to eat, drink, see or do. The legacies of imperialism are everywhere! There are lots of places around the country that have colonial roots, which we can't avoid, but what we can do is acknowledge this history and share what we've learned with others.

The world will never become a better place in the future if we don't discuss the truth about its past!

HP SAUCE

HP Sauce is a savoury brown sauce that can be found in every supermarket beside its (in my opinion) much nicer, much tastier, much less disgusting cousin tomato ketchup. As you may gather, I'm not a fan of HP Sauce. But lots and lots of other people are – 28 million bottles are sold every year! And it's a particularly British product. Indeed, 'HP' stands for the Houses of Parliament, and there's an illustration of the home of the British government on its label. Interestingly, a survey carried out at the time of the Brexit vote in 2016 found that HP Sauce was a favourite brand for people who voted for Britain to leave the European Union – a group who tend to be proudly patriotic.

HP Sauce itself is a product of the empire. It was invented in 1899 by a grocer from Nottinghamshire, who blended together some of the ingredients found in colonized lands and products that were widely available in Britain because of its colonies: dates, tamarind and cayenne spices, molasses. It added a real oomph to the rather plain British diet of the time.

Many other food manufacturers also took advantage of this new source of flavours. The company Crosse & Blackwell, which still exists today, sent an employee over with the first troops shipped out to India by the East India Company to get ideas for new products such as chutneys. Meanwhile, Worcestershire sauce, another ghastly brown concoction, might be named after an English county but is originally thought to have been an Indian recipe, reportedly brought back to Britain by an ex-governor of Bengal (in India).

Not only did British people like these condiments at home, but they wanted them overseas too. Huge numbers of bottles and jars of sauces, pickles and chutneys were exported to colonialists in the outposts of the British Empire, so that they could have a taste of home – even though the products were made from foreign ingredients. The glass bottles and jars were wrapped in paper to avoid them breaking on the long sea voyage, and until quite recently Lea & Perrins' Worcestershire sauce was still sold with a paper wrapping. If only all that HP Sauce had been lost at sea!

THE COMMONWEALTH

You may have heard people mention the Commonwealth and not been entirely sure what it is. I don't blame you! There are lots of adults who don't fully understand it either but, in short, it's a group of countries, many of which used to be part of the British Empire. Some people think this is a good thing, some think it's a bit pointless, and some think it is a terrible idea. One thing everyone can agree on, though, is that it came about directly from the British Empire.

At its height in the early 1900s the British Empire covered a quarter of the planet. But over time British colonies began to break free, starting with the USA, Canada and Australia. The modern Commonwealth was established as a way for Britain to keep some connection with these newly independent countries (although some might say that Britain wants this to protect its own interests!). The leaders of Australia, Canada,

India, the Irish Free State (now the Republic of Ireland), Newfoundland, New Zealand and South Africa attended a gathering in 1926 called the Imperial Conference. At this meeting these countries and Britain agreed that they would all be equal members within the British Empire and the term 'Commonwealth' was officially adopted to describe the community. While Britain's kings and queens in recent decades have been head of the Commonwealth, they have not always been head of state for each Commonwealth country. When India became independent, for example, it decided not to keep the British monarch as head of state – instead it has a president to do the job.

Today there are fifty-four independent countries in the Commonwealth 'family'. Most members of the Commonwealth were formerly part of the British Empire, but not all of them (for example, Rwanda). The Commonwealth is home to 2.5 billion people and includes a variety of countries, from the tiny Pacific nation of Nauru (with a population of about 10,000) to huge countries like India that have a population of over 1.4 billion). The members agree to shared values such as commitments to human rights, equality between its citizens, and democracy (a political system in which citizens can vote governments in and out through fair elections).

The Commonwealth is not like the empire in one very important way: the countries in it are free and Britain is not in charge of them. However, for some people, having a large collection of countries with a British royal at the head, even in a symbolic role, makes the Commonwealth feel a bit too, well, empirey. These critics find it particularly annoying when members of the royal family go on tours of Commonwealth countries, where they are treated in the same way as they were during the empire, such as being carried on the shoulders of locals on thrones and waving at local people from the back of open-top cars!

Nowadays, with more people aware of the truth about the British Empire, with its racism, violence and inequality, such visits don't always go down so well. The Prince and Princess of Wales recently toured the Caribbean and were met with protests from people who thought these displays were outdated, and who did not want to honour a country that had been so involved in the slave trade, which had devastated their people. In response to this, news reports claimed that Prince William and Kate are keen to address Britain's colonial past on future royal tours. King Charles III has also called for the history of the slave trade to be taught more widely in Britain and said in a speech that he was continuing to 'deepen his own understanding of slavery's enduring impact'. We are not alone on this educational journey of ours.

COCA-COLA

Great, I've got your attention! Actually this bit could just as well be called Haribo, candyfloss, Twix, Bounty or any other sweet treat. We're going to look at why these delicious teeth-rotting goodies exist – which is the story of how sugar became cheap and plentiful.

Sugar has been around in Britain for about a thousand years, but for ages it was so rare and expensive that it was only for the very rich. Even then they didn't use it like we do now – they just added a tiny bit to their food to make it more interesting. In fact, back then sugar was considered a spice!

Then came the British Empire. As we now know, in the 1600s British explorers made their way to distant islands. When they discovered these lands had lots of space for farming valuable products, they thought *We'll have that!* One of these islands was Barbados in the West Indies, and it proved a good place to grow sugar cane (a plant that sugar is produced from).

In order to make the most money from this valuable product, the British used enslaved African people to grow and produce the sugar, which was then shipped back to Britain. On the back of the suffering of the enslaved people, these sugar plantations made a lot of money. They soon spread across the Caribbean and other parts of the empire, and as sugar became more and more available the British began consuming more and more of it (and using it to sweeten their tea). But sugar was still too expensive to be available in large quantities to everyone.

One of the big changes happened in the middle of the nineteenth century, after Britain had abolished the slave trade. At this point the formerly enslaved people were so-called 'freedmen' and 'freedwomen', although the work they did on sugar plantations was still gruelling and badly paid. To understand what happened next, I need to explain something called 'sugar duty', which was a form of tax. I know that duties and taxes can sound boring, but I'll do my best to make it interesting!

Imagine if the computer games you bought with your pocket money had a duty of 10 per cent added on. This would mean that on top of paying, say, £20 for the game, you might have to pay the government an additional £2, bringing the total price to £22. This would be similar to what happened with sugar; every time someone bought sugar, the government would put a tax on it, making it more expensive to buy. This was called 'sugar duty'.

Now imagine if the government removed the computer-game duty. Suddenly the games would be cheaper, and you wouldn't have to save up so long to buy them. You'd feel a bit richer. That's what happened when the British government removed sugar duty in 1874. It meant that sugar became cheaper and even poorer people could enjoy it.

Over time people discovered other sources of sugar, such as the sugar beet plant, which can be grown in colder climates. This made sugar even cheaper again and by 1901 the average person in Britain was eating around 40 kilograms of sugar a year – that's probably more than you weigh! Jam, which is made from fruit and lots of sugar, became hugely popular because it was cheap, tasty and high in energy. Jam factories sprang up everywhere, and some of the companies established then, such as Hartley's and Wilkin & Sons, are still going strong today. Food manufacturers have also found lots of other ways to use all this cheap sugar . . . sweets and fizzy drinks!

But, believe it or not, we're actually consuming less sugar today than we did a hundred years ago. Tell that to your dentist!

CHAPTER 5

Why are British families from
so many different places?

As I have mentioned, I grew up in Wolverhampton, which is in an area of England often nicknamed the Black Country. When I was at school, a teacher asked the class if we knew why it was called that, and a classmate put up his hand and suggested it was because lots of Black and brown people lived there. We all laughed. The real explanation is thought to be the black soot that bellowed out from all the factories during and after the Industrial Revolution. But like many unintentionally funny comments, it contained some truth. The Black Country, and the wider West Midlands in which it's located, is indeed a very multicultural area, where thousands of people of different cultures, customs, beliefs and skin colours live next to each other in the wider community. Many other parts of Britain are like this too. And a major reason for that is – you guessed it – the empire!

Multiculturalism isn't a modern thing at all. There have been Black and brown people in Britain for centuries, and they came here by many different routes. Some were enslaved from countries that make up the continent of Africa. While Britain was active in the slave trade, the people who were enslaved were generally transported straight from Africa to the Caribbean and America. Because of this, lots of people seem to think there was no Black slavery in Britain itself, but it was not uncommon for slave-ship captains to bring a few enslaved people back with them from the Caribbean to sell at home. In the 1700s it was fashionable for wealthy people to have what they called an 'exotic' Black servant and British newspapers sometimes carried adverts from slave owners trying to locate 'runaways'.

Meanwhile, the East India Company liked to employ Asian sailors on their ships, because they were cheaper and harder-working than English sailors. Once they were in Britain some of these men couldn't afford the journey home and settled here, marrying white women and having families. Also, Indian and Chinese women were employed as nannies for British families on the long voyage home from the colonies and ended up staying in Britain too. These women were called *ayahs*, and a home was opened up for those who had been abandoned at the docks by English colonizers.

Although Britain was officially a Christian country, people of different religions settled here too. The first mosque was built in Britain way back in 1889 (the Shah Jahan Mosque, Woking). And it wasn't just Black and brown people who emigrated either. At one stage Ireland was a colony of Britain, and many Irish people moved here as well.

Immigrants formed communities in places where they could find work, such as by docks or in industrial areas. Some studied law, or became actors, sportsmen or doctors and nurses, such as Mary Seacole (see page 97).

During the two world wars, millions of citizens from the colonies fought and died alongside British soldiers. Then, in 1948, after the Second World War, something happened that lots of people don't know about – at least I didn't before starting to research this subject! The government passed the Nationality Act. And it was a huge deal. It basically gave everyone who lived in the colonies the right to live in Britain. At the time that was a staggering 600 million people – around nine times today's population of Britain.

In the same year a transport ship called the *Empire Windrush* arrived in London carrying 500 passengers from Jamaica. The now quite elderly people who emigrated to Britain at that time are called the 'Windrush generation'. When the passengers arrived, they did so as British citizens and they spent their first night in a hostel in Brixton in south London. Many decided to stay and settle there, which is how Brixton became home to one of the most famous Black communities in Britain.

Another important thing for immigration happened in 1948 (yes, it was an eventful year!). The National Health Service, or NHS, was founded. Many immigrants found jobs within the new NHS, taking on all sorts of roles from doctors to porters. It remains a highly

multicultural organization to this day, with 44 per cent of NHS medical staff being from a Black, Asian or ethnic minority background (an ethnic minority is a group of people with a shared language, culture and history who live in a country where most people have a different language, culture and history). This was sadly illustrated during the early months of the Covid pandemic, when a large number of Black and brown hospital staff died.

Sometimes, the way we hear people in power talking about immigration today, it might seem as though Black and brown people arrived in Britain without permission. But, as you can see, this is simply not true! What is true is that not long after passing the Nationality Act in 1948, the British government decided it had been a mistake. There was an intense racist backlash, which was sometimes violent, with lots of white Britons not wanting to work and live alongside brown and Black immigrants. So politicians made new laws to undo the generosity of the 1948 Nationality Act, and today it's much more difficult for people from the former empire or Commonwealth to come and live and work in Britain. But it was because of this act passing in the first place – and of course because of the empire – that Britain is home to so many people from so many different cultures, religions, races, nationalities and backgrounds.

In other words, the reason Britain is a multicultural country is because it had a multicultural empire.

But immigration is an issue that can make people very upset and angry ('flammable' is a good adjective here – it means easily bursting into flames). Some Britons feel that Britain doesn't have enough space for new people. Some worry that immigrants are expensive for the government to look after. Some white people in Britain also feel that they have more of a claim to the country than people of colour. You might hear them making claims such as 'immigrants are taking our jobs'. Perhaps this hatred exists, in part, because many of us don't know the history of people of colour in Britain. Maybe if these people knew that Black and brown people have been here for centuries, they would feel differently. Or maybe if they understood that the people who came here had deep links, going back hundreds of years, to the British Empire, it might help make the discussion kinder and fairer. It might also go a small way to stopping the racism faced by immigrants in this country.

Now, I wish this wasn't the case, but if you are someone who is not white, there is a chance that you might get told by a racist person at some point in your life to 'go back to where you came from'. I very much hope this never happens to you, and I hope that the more people learn about the true history of Britain's multiculturalism, the kinder they will be. But, just in case, here's how I like to respond to those comments:

> What, you mean Wolverhampton? Sure, could you pay my train fare?

Or, if you'd rather use the wise words of a Sri Lankan writer called Ambalavaner Sivanandan, you could say:

> We are here because you were there.

FINGERPRINTING

Where do you think fingerprinting was invented? Hands up! Let me see all ten of your prints! Yes, you at the back in the blue T-shirt. 'Scotland Yard?' you say? Ah, the police headquarters! No, but a good guess. You? '221B Baker Street?' Ah, where Sherlock Holmes lived! Another very good guess. But, my dear Watson, the truth is not quite so elementary. The practice of fingerprinting was actually born in India in the 1800s. And the reasons for it starting there, rather than in Britain, are pretty interesting (and also pretty racist).

These days when you want to identify someone, we have DNA tests and clever technology. But back in the 1800s there was no good way of proving someone's identity. This was a particular problem for the police, who couldn't easily tell whether the people they caught were repeat offenders, impersonating someone else or entirely innocent. One solution was to measure every part of the criminal's body - even the width of their ears -

and keep these measurements on record in case they were arrested again, but this was very time-consuming and left lots of room for error. Officers were also trained to be good at recognizing faces, but, as you can imagine, this was also not reliable and often didn't count as strong enough evidence in a court room.

Meanwhile, over in colonial India, British officials were also keen to find a way to identify people - not criminals, just ordinary people. They felt they needed to keep tabs on the Indian population in order to rule over them better. They found it hard to distinguish between brown-skinned people - which is really racist. It was also widely believed that Indians were naturally dishonest - another really racist attitude. And this led the British to feel that they couldn't trust the Indian population to correctly identify themselves.

The colonialists faced another challenge in that a large section of the Indian population was illiterate, which meant they could not read or write. Indeed, for centuries, instead of signing their names, there had been a tradition of Indian people marking documents by using a finger dipped in ink. A British official in India had a breakthrough when he realized that these fingerprints were unique to each person. This meant you could use the markings of a fingerprint to identify someone. However, this form of identification still wasn't much use – imagine how long it would take to compare two sets of fingerprints by eye! This was done until the 1800s, when a system was developed that helped officials easily match a set of prints taken from someone with prints they already had on file.

It took much longer to introduce any kind of fingerprinting system in Britain because British people did not like officials keeping tabs on them like that. However, the police were very keen on using it for criminals. And finally, in 1902, the very first criminal trial in Britain relied on fingerprint evidence. Was the case about a famous murder, a grand robbery or a dastardly deception? No, it was about a man stealing a few billiard balls (which are similar to snooker balls). Perhaps not one for Sherlock Holmes!

KEW GARDENS

Kew Gardens are among London's most famous visitor attractions, right up there alongside Big Ben and Madame Tussauds and that confusingly popular M&M's store in Leicester Square. They are situated quite far from the centre of the city though, which is unsurprising as they're 320 acres large. That's roughly the size of 226 football pitches!

Today people go there to relax in the lovely gardens, and to marvel at exotic plants in greenhouses. And that is what people did in the nineteenth century too. But back then Kew Gardens also had another important role. Certain plants and crops became very valuable in the 1800s for imperialists, and with the help of Kew Gardens Britain was able to make a lot of money from them. For example:

- The experts at Kew helped build up a massive tea industry in India.
- They took the rubber plants that grew in

South America and transplanted them to what is now known as Malaysia. And if you're stunned to discover that rubber, the material that makes up bicycle tyres and hot-water bottles, comes from a plant, you're not alone. I would have found it less surprising to discover that Xboxes grow on trees. But it's true: some rubber is produced artificially in factories, but lots of it is also made from sap that's naturally occurring in certain trees. Rubber can also be extracted from some types of dandelions! Who knew?!

• Kew transferred cinchona trees from South America to plantations around the British Empire . . . Wait! What on earth is cinchona? In the nineteenth century it was discovered that the cinchona tree contained a substance called quinine in its bark, and quinine was found to treat malaria, a very serious disease carried by mosquitoes that has killed tens of millions of people. As malaria was a danger to many in British colonies, the British wanted to get their hands on as much of this medicine as they could. Kew's experts collected samples of the valuable plants from their native countries and brought them to Kew Gardens, where the best plant experts in Britain worked. The plants were then studied. Some were planted at Kew, and some were sent abroad. Britain managed to transplant enough cinchona around the world to protect its imperialists from the worst effects of malaria. The medicine they produced is part of the reason British imperialists were able to conquer parts of West Africa in the 1800s, a part of the world where malaria was a frequent cause of death.

Records show that Kew was also involved in sending cinchona and tobacco to Saint Helena in the South Atlantic; mahogany (often used to make brown furniture) to India; rubber to West Africa; coffee from Liberia (a country in West Africa) to the East and West Indies; tea plants to Jamaica; cork oaks to the Punjab; pineapples to the Straits Settlements in South-East Asia; and oranges, bananas, almonds and much, much more elsewhere.

You might be wondering how these exotic plants that were so used to hot climates survived in Britain. Well, the experts at Kew were able to copy the natural environments of many of the plants. Initially, most of the plants came from India's Calcutta Botanic Gardens, and so glasshouses at Kew Gardens were kept very hot to match the climate in India. The famous Palm House was designed to offer visitors a taste of the empire. One newspaper journalist at the time described feeling that 'a tiger might start out from among tree-ferns, a boa-constrictor might be climbing the trunk of that cocoa-nut palm'. Now that would be an exciting day out!

THE JUNGLE BOOK

The Jungle Book is a collection of stories published in the nineteenth century by the English author Rudyard Kipling. It features characters such as tiger Shere Khan, Baloo the bear and 'man-cub' Mowgli, a boy who is brought up in the jungle by wolves. The tales are set in a forest in India, and you may have seen one of the many film adaptations, or perhaps even read the stories, originally published in 1894.

Kipling was born in British-ruled India to English parents, and he spent his early childhood there. He saw India as a magical place, and the country provided the setting for many of his stories. Kipling became a celebrity in Britain because of his writing. As well as stories, he also wrote the poem 'If –', which is regularly named the most popular poem in Britain. It's so famous that lines from it are printed above the players' entrance to Wimbledon's Centre Court. And Kipling was a big fan of the British Empire. A really big fan. If British imperialism was a pop band today, he would probably buy a ticket for every single concert, send them tons of fan mail, and start a TikTok channel to film himself dancing to their songs.

Kipling and Baden-Powell (who we heard about earlier on pages 27–29) were friends, and when Baden-Powell wanted to extend Scouting to younger boys *The Jungle Book* provided the framework for the activities and names of his

Wolf Cub club ('Cubs'). Baden-Powell wrote to Kipling in 1916: 'I want to enthuse them through your Mowgli and his animal friends of *The Jungle Book.*' The Cubs form packs, perform a Grand Howl, and are led by Akela, the Indian wolf.

Since it is very well known that Kipling was hugely pro-empire, some people see *The Jungle Book* as an allegory about the empire. An allegory is a hidden story within a story, usually offering a moral or lesson. So while some people see *The Jungle Book* as simply telling the tale of Mowgli, an Indian boy who is raised by wolves and learns how to be independent from jungle animals, others think it contains another message. In this way of looking at it, *The Jungle Book* is really about British imperialism in India. Mowgli, who represents the British, ends up ruling the jungle in the same way that the white colonialists did with India. One critic describes Mowgli as 'behaving towards the beasts as the British do to the Indians'.

But this doesn't mean that you shouldn't enjoy *The Jungle Book* any more, so please don't worry. This is just one way of looking at it. Other people disagree, and think, for instance, that the story is actually about courage, abandonment and belonging. (In real life the young Kipling was sent to Britain without his parents and was very unhappy, and so might have felt a bit like an orphan himself.) And some of his writing expresses mixed, complicated feelings about empire.

We'll never know Kipling's true and full intentions, and there's certainly no harm in reading his stories if you enjoy them. You can form your own opinions about *any* books – whether they are written by Rudyard Kipling or anyone else (including this one!).

CHAPTER 6
But I wasn't even there!

Scattered throughout these pages are examples of things, places and activities that had their origins in the British Empire, but imperialism does not just have physical legacies. Our attitudes and beliefs have also been shaped by the empire – yes, that's right, the way you and I and the country as a whole think has also been impacted by it. Now, our thoughts may not be as lively as London Zoo or as messy as fingerprinting or as gross as HP Sauce or as tasty as sweets, but they're just as important. (I'm joking, of course. What could be as important as sweets?)

Here are some examples of beliefs that you may recognize either in adults you know, or in things you have seen or read, or perhaps even in yourself, which might have come from this period of history:

Exceptionalism and jingoism

'Exceptionalism' is a pleasing six-syllable word. It's the idea that Britain is different from other countries. And not just different but better. Special! And, as a result, Britain doesn't need to obey the rules like everyone else. (We'll get to 'jingoism' in a moment.)

You probably know someone at school who is like this – someone who thinks they can get away with anything because they are special. Maybe they're really loud in class, or they show off about how well they're doing all the time. Annoying, aren't they? Well, in some ways Britain can sometimes act just like that annoying kid at school.

Think of it this way. Britain is a small country with a tiny fraction of the world's population, and yet it ruled over a quarter of the planet! Britain ran the biggest empire in human history! In some ways it's no surprise that our nation thinks it's better than others. And who doesn't want to be special? I must have spent half my childhood trying to demonstrate how I was better and more special than my brothers and sisters and therefore didn't need to obey the same rules. But exceptionalism can be dangerous when it comes to countries.

I want to be clear here that I don't think there's anything wrong with being proud of Britain. There are lots of things to be proud of. From its writers, like Shakespeare and Malorie Blackman, to the Premier League, its pop music and not to mention the beautiful countryside

and historic cities that people from all over the world travel to visit. There are also the facts that Britain eventually abolished slavery and encouraged other nations to do so, that Britain defeated the Nazis, and is now a fairly tolerant multicultural society. (As I've explored in this book, those facts are more complicated than they first appear, but they're still achievements we can be proud of.)

But being proud of British achievements is different to believing that Britain is better than other countries and doesn't need to obey the same rules as a result. When it comes to countries, a belief in one's own exceptionalism can lead to extreme pride, which can pit people against each other in a dangerous way. This extreme pride is sometimes called 'jingoism'. This is the belief that your country is always the best, and this can lead to citizens feeling powerful and

superior. This is bad because this feeling often comes at the expense of other people.

Think back to that annoying person at school. Now, there's no problem with them being proud of their own achievements, but if this leads to them putting other people down to feel better about themselves, then there's an issue. And, as we've seen, a lot of harm can come when one nation believes they are better than others . . .

Racism

The belief that Britain is special and superior can also lead to racism. Now, Britain is certainly not alone in suffering from racism. It exists everywhere, including in countries that have never had empires. Nevertheless, as British-Indian writer Salman Rushdie (another person who I think we should be very proud of) once put it, 'four centuries of being told that you are superior' to brown and Black people 'leave their stain'. That stain might not be visible, like the ketchup or HP Sauce (eww) you've dribbled down your shirt during lunch, but it's there.

British imperialists formed all sorts of strange insulting ideas about different races and these strange insulting ideas have passed down the generations. For instance, they made absurd claims about what specific things brown and Black groups were good and bad at. They recorded 'facts' about the people they colonized, which ranged from wrong to utterly wrong. For example, they claimed that Sikh people were warrior-like (as you can tell from my photo on page 194, some Sikhs really aren't built for fighting!). They suggested that Indians tended to have 'enlarged spleens' caused by malaria, which meant they were more likely than white people to die when hit (this was often used as a legal defence to get British people off charges of murder against Indians). They claimed that African people would not work if given a choice. They argued that other races were lazy or cowardly. No one making such generalizations about millions of people across entire continents would be taken seriously today, but during empire this kind of white supremacy was common. Unfortunately some of these absurd and offensive ideas have filtered down into modern society. Many harmful stereotypes (oversimplified labels) that began in the days of the empire are still around today.

Cleverness

Less seriously there's also the British attitude towards cleverness. Have you ever heard someone – maybe even you – being described as too clever for their own good? Or been told to stop being such a smarty-pants? Perhaps you remember this line from the film of Roald Dahl's *Matilda*: 'A girl does not get anywhere by acting intelligent.' These examples all show a traditional British attitude towards intelligence. Mainly that if you're clever, you should just keep quiet about it!

I don't know of any other country that thinks like this. I believe this British attitude came about during the days of the empire, when the men in charge were often posh but not always very clever. These men from the upper classes believed that they were the only ones who could run things properly; they thought they were 'born to rule'.

Going abroad to an exotic land full of money-making opportunities was thought to be a decent job, and lots of men wanted to do it, but it often wasn't the cleverest men who were picked for the task. This is because some of the people in charge at the height of the empire decided that the ideal candidates to work in the colonies were people who pretty much did what they were told without grumbling about it. Clever men who thought for themselves and questioned things were seen as dangerous, because they might think things like: *Hey, what are we doing here?* and *What right do we have to invade and colonize this country?* Some very clever men who worked in the colonies, like the writer George Orwell, did question things. In *The Road to Wigan Pier* he wrote: 'All over India, there are Englishmen who secretly loathe the system of which they are part.'

This idea that cleverness is not something to be encouraged has stuck around. So what should we do about this legacy of attitudes and beliefs that continue to shape our thoughts today? Well, being aware of them is a very good start! Once you're aware, you can start to challenge them. In the next chapter, we'll talk about some practical ways you can do this.

SHAMPOO

There once lived an extraordinary man called Dean Mahomed. An Indian Muslim, he lived from 1759–1851, and worked for the East India Company (them again!). While working for the company, he became friends with one of the officers, who then brought him over from India to the British Isles as his companion.

Over here in Britain, Dean Mahomed wrote the first book ever written by an Indian person in English (it wasn't well written, but never mind). He also married an Irish woman at a time when there were very few marriages between white and non-white people. The couple eventually moved to London, where they set up a restaurant serving Indian food – the very first curry house in Britain.

I know what you're thinking. *This is all very interesting, and I love poppadoms, so hats off to this guy for inventing the curry house. But what about the shampoo?* Well, Dean Mahomed was a businessman and he was also canny – he knew that English society was fascinated by what it saw as the 'exotic East'. So after the restaurant he set up a new business, opening a kind of bathhouse (a building containing public baths for people to use) in the seaside resort of Brighton. He called himself a 'shampooing surgeon'.

A what? Well, the word 'shampoo' comes from the Hindi word *champi*, meaning 'massage', which, in turn, means applying pressure to muscles and joints of the human body, usually to relieve pain or tension. And the 'surgeon' bit? So, in those days medical professionals weren't licensed as strictly as they are today, and people could go around calling themselves doctors and surgeons with little training. Dean Mahomed probably thought calling himself a surgeon made him sound impressive, when actually he was just good at giving massages.

Nevertheless, his shampooing was a big hit!

The king of England at the time, George IV, even became a customer, as well as many other fashionable Victorians. For a while the shampooing surgeon's bathhouse in Brighton was the place to be (even though a member of Dean's team once snapped a man's arm during a massage, resulting in it being amputated!).

Dean Mahomed was a pioneer, and at a time of great racism he didn't let his Indian identity hold him back. In fact, he used it to his advantage. In my eyes that's hugely impressive. And he helped popularize the word 'shampoo'. The meaning has changed over the years. At first it meant, as a verb, 'to massage'. Then it started to mean, more precisely, as the *Oxford English Dictionary* explains, 'to wash and rub with some cleaning agent'. Eventually it also became a noun, referring to the liquid soap you use to wash your hair. I told you etymology could be interesting!

WEMBLEY STADIUM

Have you ever been to Wembley Stadium? You can visit this huge venue to watch football (it hosts many of the biggest games) or to see your favourite singer in concert (like Harry Styles or Taylor Swift). A hundred years ago, however, you might have come to Wembley to see something very different: a life-size sculpture of the Prince of Wales and his horse - made out of BUTTER!*

The original Wembley Stadium - which was then called the Empire Stadium - was built for the British Empire Exhibition in 1924, and the unusual exhibit of the Prince of Wales was one of the sights on offer there. The idea was

to show how large, varied and impressive the empire was. The exhibition showed off many of its different colonies, and each one was given its own pavilion designed in the typical architecture of the country. Every pavilion was populated by its citizens demonstrating their traditions and displaying local crafts and produce.

For instance, the West Africa area was a village of thatched huts, featuring West Africans weaving and carving. Hong Kong, meanwhile, had an entire Chinese shopping street, complete with traders offering ivory knick-knacks, fabrics and toys. Burma's pavilion was a copy of a famous Buddhist temple and was reached by a wooden bridge. There were also exhibits of weapons and engineering breakthroughs, rodeo shows, concerts, a funfair and a specially built railway to take visitors round the enormous site.

It sounds rather exciting, doesn't it? The visitors of the time certainly thought so. A whopping

17 million people turned up for the exhibition in 1924. That's around the same number of people who would get to see Harry Styles play at Wembley if he played for 188 nights in a row! It was so successful, in fact, that the exhibition was put on again the next year.

Wembley eventually became England's national stadium, going on to host the Summer Olympics of 1948, and many football matches, including the famous 1966 World Cup final, which England won! Then in 2000 the stadium was completely rebuilt, reopening in 2007 with its now famous arch towering above it. So while the stadium today isn't the same one that was built for the Empire Exhibition of 1924, it wouldn't exist without it.

*Oh, I nearly forgot to explain what that butter sculpture was all about! Well, one of the engineering developments on show at the exhibition was refrigeration, which was revolutionary at the time as it allowed meat and dairy products from around the world to be transported to Britain without going off (see page 54). To show just how great their refrigeration was, the Canadians carved the butter sculpture and displayed it in a huge refrigerated case. For the 1925 exhibition the Australians created an even larger butter sculpture, with a scene from their recent 4–1 win over England in the Ashes, a cricket tournament. Thank goodness there wasn't a power cut!

PLACE NAMES

The construction of Wembley Stadium was a massive project, and along with the building itself came 15 miles of walkways and new streets. These new roads were named by Rudyard Kipling, who we met earlier on page 147.

If you recall, Rudyard Kipling was a massive fan of the British Empire. And considering the circumstances, it's not surprising that there was an imperial theme to the street names he chose. They included Dominion Way (a word used by the British to describe a type of colony), Atlantic Slope (the ocean dividing Britain from some of its colonies) and, yes, Empire Way. Though it's not just in Wembley that one can find such imperial legacies in place names. They are everywhere. For example:

- The Kop is a stand in Liverpool's Anfield football stadium. It is named after Spion Kop, which was the location of a famous battle during the South African War, one of the biggest colonial conflicts.

- In Wandsworth, south London, street names include Cabul (now Kabul), Candahar (now Kandahar) and Khyber, which are places in Afghanistan and refer to foreign cities that became well known as a result of an 1800s imperial conflict.

- Bristol has Colston Street, as well as other sites named in honour of its most infamous slave trader, Edward Colston (see page 113). There are also streets named after other lesser-known men involved in the slave trade: Elton Road, Winterstoke Road, Tyndalls Avenue and Farr Lane.

- In Liverpool, the legacy of the slave trade can be found in names including Cunliffe Street, Ashton Street and Blundell Street.

All these names might not be around forever, though. In recent years some local councils have been investigating the background of their controversial street names and sometimes changing them to better reflect the world today. For example, there was a road in Southall in west London which honoured Major-General Henry Havelock, who is well known for fighting Indians rebelling against British rule in 1857. Southall is home to a high number of Sikhs and about half the people who live there are of Indian background. The road was recently renamed after the founder of Sikhism, Guru Nanak. In 2020, a venue called Colston Hall in Bristol – yet another tribute to Edward Colston – changed its name to Bristol Beacon.

And then there's Pero's Bridge in Bristol. This is a relatively new bridge, and when it was opened in 1999 it was named after an African man called Pero Jones, who was transported to Bristol as an enslaved person in 1790. Pero represents the thousands of African people who were enslaved by Bristol's traders, and whose names have been lost to history.

POKÉMON CARDS

Of course, Pokémon cards didn't exist in the 1800s! However, what happened at that time paved the way for them to be invented. And the tobacco industry played an important role.

Now, we haven't talked very much about tobacco, even though it was an important product of the empire, alongside things such as tea, sugar and cotton. Smoking is very dangerous and addictive and even kills, so it might be surprising to hear how popular it has been throughout history. At the end of the 1800s tobacco was a highly prized product that was grown by enslaved people on plantations in America (and elsewhere) and imported to Europe. There were hundreds of cigarette companies in Britain alone, and, following the example of some companies in the USA, these brands started including little cards in their packets of cigarettes. The practical purpose of these cards was to keep the cardboard packets stiff to protect the cigarettes inside, but the companies also realized they could use them to get people to buy more of their products. They made the cards collectable, printing different designs on them to encourage people to keep buying the cigarettes.

In Britain, many of these designs had an imperial theme, like flags of the colonies, industries of the empire, heroes of the empire, Indian army regiments and so on. For people who didn't read newspapers these cards were their main source of information about the empire. John Player cigarettes issued a 'British Empire' series of cards in 1904 and a series of cards on 'Military Uniforms of the British Empire Overseas' in 1938. Tobacco manufacturer W. D. & H. O. Wills published a 'Builders of the Empire' series in 1898, 'Arms of the British Empire' in 1910, 'Governors General of India' in 1911, 'Indian Regiments' in 1912 and 'Picturesque People of the Empire' in 1929. Meanwhile, Lambert & Butler had a set advertising Rhodesia (see page 115) as a destination to move to in 1938, probably influenced by the fact that the company purchased its tobacco from the British colony there.

Cigarettes are far less popular these days, but collectable trading cards remain big business. In

America, cards featuring baseball players were massively popular throughout the twentieth century – one rare card of a player called Honus Wagner sold for over $6 million (which is nearly £5 million)! And then, in the late 1990s, came Pokémon. Their Trading Card Game is hugely successful – a mind-boggling 43 billion cards have been produced since it was launched. The designs may be different now, but the principle of the trading cards remains the same. As those cute little pocket monsters have it, gotta catch 'em all!

CHAPTER 7
What can I do?

I feel excited that, through this book, young readers like you will have the kind of information about colonialism that I didn't learn until my forties. If I had known even half these things when I was younger, it would have changed my feelings about Britain and my place in it, probably for the better. We are united by this complex imperial history; there are few ethnic groups that were not influenced by the British Empire. This is not just Black history, or brown history, or the history of minority ethnic people – it is also white history.

But if you're anything like me, you might also be feeling alarmed at some of the new information you've come across. You might be distressed about the intense ill-treatment and violence that happened during the British Empire. You might also be upset at the racism that was part of imperialism and which continues as its legacy. And you might be angry that this history is not better known or better taught. If you can, please try to channel this emotion in positive ways. If you've read all this and think you might want to help spread knowledge about this stolen history, if you feel that the truth about the British Empire has been silenced for too long, if you want to encourage constructive conversation instead of angry arguing, here are some suggestions of things you could do.

Ask awkward (but polite) questions at school

The British Empire is being taught more than it used to be. The national curriculum states that teachers must cover 'political power, industry and Empire' in Britain between 1745 and 1901 for ages eleven to fourteen. And although academies and private schools don't have to follow the national curriculum, lots of teachers in these schools are trying to teach it as well. Also, the Welsh government has decided to make the teaching of colonialism and Black history compulsory in its schools.

The reason this change is happening (even if it has been very slow) is because parents, teachers and pupils like you have spent years asking awkward questions.

Questions like:

Why do we not hear more about how imperial troops and money helped us win two world wars?

And:

Why do we celebrate so many slave owners in our national monuments and statues?

And if you're being taught about the Tudors yet again:

Is it true that there were Black Britons in the court of Henry VII, and why haven't we heard about them before?

And:

If we live in such a multicultural country, why are there so few writers of colour on our curriculums?

It's important to be polite when challenging teachers.

First, they don't generally set the curriculum, so if they haven't taught you about these things, it's usually not their fault! Also, as we've learned, the topic of the British Empire often gets people hot and bothered, and there's no point raising the temperature any further.

But by asking these questions and showing you're keen to learn more, you can make a difference.

Ask awkward (but polite) questions at museums

The superhero film *Black Panther* has become one of the most successful films of all time. It features a scene where a character turns up at a building that looks rather like the British Museum and informs a

museum director that he will take certain African artefacts off her hands. The director responds by stating that the items are not for sale, which provokes the response:

How do you think your ancestors got these? Do you think they paid a fair price? Or did they take it . . . like they took everything else?

The character then takes the artefacts back from the museum.

To be clear, this is not behaviour I encourage or approve of. It would definitely get you into a lot of trouble in any museum. But you could learn a lot by engaging museum workers in conversations about imperial 'loot'. Your conversations will likely reveal that there are a wide range of opinions out there about what should be done about it. Some museums such as the British Museum generally don't want to give very much back, but other institutions are making efforts to do so.

Aberdeen University has returned a Benin bronze (a type of sculpture that decorated the royal palace of the

Kingdom of Benin in what is now Edo State, Nigeria), and London's Horniman Museum has promised to do the same with artefacts from Benin. Manchester Museums recently returned forty-three sacred and ceremonial objects to Indigenous Australians, with the first artefacts being formally handed back to members of the indigenous Gangalidda Garawa group during a ceremony at Manchester Museum. And there are many more examples. Progress is slow, but change is happening. And it all starts with questions and conversations.

Prepare snappy comebacks

Sometimes when you're debating with someone, it's hard to come up with clever replies on the spot. But it's a good idea to have some up your sleeve for when you start having conversations with people about the empire. There are a few classic arguments that people tend to make in favour of the empire, which I hope, having read this book, you realize aren't necessarily true or fair.

For example, one thing people often say in these conversations is:

> But Britain abolished slavery!

You could reply:

> That's true, and that was a good thing, but Haiti abolished it long before us. We also dominated the global slave trade for long periods and sent more than 3 million people from various countries in Africa across the Atlantic and continued dealing with slave-grown cotton after abolition!

Another claim you might come across is:

> But Britain gave lots of good things to India, like the railways!

You could reply:

> The railways were actually built to benefit the British, not the Indians!

And then, with a gently sarcastic tone, add:

> But, yes, they were kind enough to leave them behind when they had finished colonizing the country.

OK, so these aren't that snappy. I'm sure you can do better!

The key is to read and be well informed – which is why I have included a list at the back of this book if you want to learn more . . .

Ask your school if you can have a debate about reparations

Reparation is the process of making amends for a wrong that has been done. When people discuss reparations in relation to empire, they are talking about how to give compensation to colonized countries for the harms of the past. As we know, talking about these topics is a great way to spread knowledge and ensure people know the truth about Britain's history. You could suggest a debate at your school, discussing whether former imperial countries should pay compensation to those they have harmed in the

past. Some people think that this is a necessary step to recognizing that colonialism and slavery have done long-lasting damage and still affect people today – for instance, through racism. A different view is that people today should not have to pay for what their ancestors did long ago. While Britain has yet to start having the conversation, Germany has already paid out some reparations. It recently paid the African country of Namibia €1.1 billion (which is around £950 million). And the Germans even have a special word for the process of coming to terms with their past, and I bet it's the longest word you have read today, or even this year. It's *Vergangenheitsaufarbeitung*. (A high five to you if you manage to use that in a debate!)

But is £950 million enough?

It's difficult to calculate how much should be paid, who should pay and who gets the money. Here's a good fact to get a debate started: estimates for how much America/the Western world should pay for its involvement in the slave trade range from $10 trillion to $777 trillion (that's anywhere from £8.2 trillion to £639 trillion).

Another essential fact: when Britain started to gradually abolish slavery across the empire in 1833 it paid £20 million in compensation to slave owners – worth about £17 billion in today's money. That's £17,000,000,000. This amounted to 40 per cent of the government's whole national annual budget at the time, and was the government's largest loan of the entire nineteenth century. Enough money, according to one economic historian, to pay for a 'medium-sized war'. It was such a large sum of money that the British government only finished paying it off in 2015. In contrast, how much money did the enslaved and their offspring get for the ill-treatment, suffering, torture and death they had endured for multiple generations? £0.

Another potential question is, can a country or family even pay their way out of their involvement in such a painful history?

If you experience racism, talk about it

If you experience racism, please do tell a grown-up and ask for help if you need it. I know that it can be tempting to just try to ignore these things, especially if it happens to you quite a lot, or if you feel that you don't want to cause trouble. But the only way society will change is if racism is challenged. And nobody deserves to be spoken to or treated in this way.

Be an ally

This basically means be supportive. So even if you are a white British person, and have never experienced racism or discrimination yourself, you can still be on the side of those who have. If you look at photos of a Black Lives Matter protest, you will see white people there too – they are being allies. But you don't have to go on protests; listening to other people and trying to understand their different experience is important too. Listening can be an incredibly powerful thing to do.

Build your own statue

Or paint a picture. Or make a film. Or write a story. In general, I think building things and creating art is often better than tearing things down. I think some of the best responses to our complex and sometimes difficult imperial history have been creative and artistic ones. A few years before the Edward Colston statue was pulled down in Bristol, an artwork appeared on the ground beside it, showing dozens of figures packed tightly as if on board an eighteenth-century slave ship. If you search online for 'Colston anti-slavery art installation', you can see a picture of it. It's a very powerful reminder of the terrible way that Colston made his money. Art like this invites the person seeing it to think and to ask questions.

And, as I hope this book has made clear, I believe asking questions is the most important thing we can all do.

FURTHER READING

Black and British: A Short, Essential History and *Black and British: An Illustrated History* by David Olusoga (Macmillan Children's Books, 2020 and 2021 respectively)

City of Stolen Magic by Nazneen Ahmed Pathak (Puffin Books, 2023)

Black In Time by Alison Hammond and E. L. Norry (Puffin Books, 2022)

This Book is Anti-Racist by Tiffany Jewell (Frances Lincoln Children's Books, 2020)

The Extraordinary Life of Mahatma Gandhi by Chitra Soundar (Puffin Books, 2019)

The Extraordinary Life of Mary Seacole by Naida Redgrave (Puffin Books, 2019)

Me And White Supremacy (YA Edition) by Layla F. Saad (Quercus, 2022)

PRAISE FOR *EMPIRELAND*

Winner of the 2022 British Book Award for Narrative Non-Fiction

'*Empireland* takes a perfectly judged approach to its contentious but necessary subject'
Jonathan Coe

'I only wish this book had been around when I was at school'
Sadiq Khan, Mayor of London

'We are unconscious citizens of Empireland: empire made us, whether we realize it or not . . . The history is on Sanghera's side. The facts speak for themselves'
Telegraph

ABOUT THE AUTHOR

Sathnam Sanghera was born to Punjabi immigrant parents in Wolverhampton in 1976. He entered the education system unable to speak English, but went on to graduate from Christ's College, Cambridge, with a first-class degree in English Language and Literature. He has been shortlisted for the Costa Book Awards twice, for his memoir *The Boy With the Topknot* and his novel *Marriage Material*. *Empireland* was a *Sunday Times* bestseller that was longlisted for the Baillie Gifford Prize for Non-Fiction, and won the Nibbies Book of the Year for Non-Fiction: Narrative in 2022. He lives in London.

ABOUT THE ILLUSTRATOR

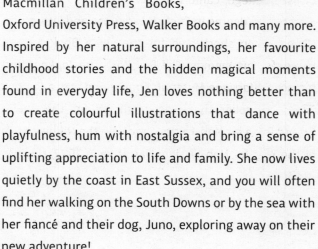

Jen Khatun is a children's book illustrator of Bangladeshi/ Indian heritage, who grew up in the beautiful, quaint city of Winchester. She has published work with Macmillan Children's Books, Oxford University Press, Walker Books and many more. Inspired by her natural surroundings, her favourite childhood stories and the hidden magical moments found in everyday life, Jen loves nothing better than to create colourful illustrations that dance with playfulness, hum with nostalgia and bring a sense of uplifting appreciation to life and family. She now lives quietly by the coast in East Sussex, and you will often find her walking on the South Downs or by the sea with her fiancé and their dog, Juno, exploring away on their new adventure!

INDEX